MW00328059

Success
without
Guilt

Success without Guilt

Following God's Lead Down the Path to Personal Achievement

Robert Strand

New Leaf Press

First printing: February 1998

Copyright © 1997 by New Leaf Press. All rights reserved. No part of this book may be used or reproduced in any manner whatsoever without written permission of the publisher, except in the case of brief quotations in articles and reviews. For information write: New Leaf Press, P.O. Box 726, Green Forest, AR 72638.

ISBN: 0-89221-372-8
Library of Congress Number: 97-75891

Cover by Left Coast Design, Portland, Oregon.

Unless otherwise noted, all Scripture is from the New International Version of the Bible.

Printed in the United States of America.

Dedicated . . .

to all the people in my life who have shared secrets of success with me. I must begin with my deceased father, John, who taught me to never give up, and my mother, Ruth, who was always ready with the assurance that whatever you wanted to do, you could do it. Also . . . my wife Donna, who thought up the title and gave the encouragement to write this book, and to teachers, mentors, and role models who have made a difference in my life. Thanks!

Contents

Contents

A Word or Two to Begin With . . .

Success is one of the most exciting human concepts which we must learn to handle! It's easy to assume that everybody wants to be a success in life and living. After all, isn't the search and work for success part of our human condition? But if we begin to scratch beneath the surface of many people . . . we discover a very common human problem. Many people are struggling with success, some have guilt about success . . . theirs or others. Why? One of the first problems to overcome comes out of our socialization. We have been taught that somehow too much success is bad, that people who experience success somehow are changed for the worst, that the Bible is against people becoming successful. And much more of the same type of rationalization.

Let's take another look at this subject of success from a different perspective. But before we do . . . understand that the most complete book on success has already been written by the most exciting author who has ever penned anything to be read by others. The book is the Bible and the author is God, through the inspiration which was given by the Holy Spirit, through holy men of God who wrote

the inspired thoughts of God for our human consump-
tion.

God is not anti-success! God is pro-success! The problem comes with how people have achieved success and
what they have done with their success. That is the problem from a biblical perspective. And don't forget as we
work our way through this book:

> GOD WANTS YOU TO BE A SUCCESS!
> THE MORE IMPORTANT QUESTION IS:
> Do YOU want to be
> a success in your living?

Without successful people there are no jobs, no surplus from which to build churches, no new industries, no
new concepts, no retirements, no ways or means with
which to build a nation! God is in the success business,
not in the failure business. Success is the result of following well-defined principles. It is not luck nor is it an accident.

What is "success"? You will discover that there are
about as many definitions of success as there are people
who write about "success." In its broadest definition, to
succeed at anything is to: be fruitful, be effective, do well,
bear fruit, click, hit, catch, attain a goal, achieve one's
aim, to be triumphant, avail, win, prosper, make good,
find fulfillment, move up, come into possession of, have
a happy outcome, to advance, to be completed, thriv-
ing, and well-received! Notice, not once did I spell success like this: "$ucce$$"! To define success in terms of
money only is to find the very narrowest of meanings.
Success may mean more money to you . . . but not necessarily. The opposite of success is failure, missing, disaster, defeat, downfall, or collapse. Not a pretty picture!

We will search for the biblical concepts which God has ordained that should mark what success is, how it is to be achieved, and how it is to be used. There is a correct, biblical, godly way in which you can experience and work for success without guilt!

> This is what the Lord says: "For I know the plans I have for you," declares the Lord, "plans to prosper you and not to harm you, plans to give you hope and a future" (Jer. 29:10-11).

The Truest Meaning of Success

Success is a journey . . . not a destination!

Okay, so what really is "success"? The answer depends on who is defining success. Let's begin with a story.

Joseph, a second-grader, shoved while boarding the school bus, suffered a two-inch cut on his cheek which required an emergency room visit for stitches. Back at school, after that important stop, while at recess, he collided with another boy and knocked out two front teeth and a trip to the dentist. At the afternoon recess, while sliding on the ice, he fell and broke his wrist. Later at the hospital, for the second time that day, his father noticed Joseph clutching a quarter in his good hand and asked him about it.

Joseph said, "I found it on the ground when I fell. This is the first quarter I ever found. This sure is my lucky day!"

Let's begin at the beginning . . . Genesis 1:1. Before you are out of the second verse, God is already at work bringing order and purpose out of chaos. If there were no chaos, there would be no need for order, therefore

13

chaos is foundational to the existence of our universe. The very first creational act brought light into the darkness and eventually light gives way to life. But without the light first, there would be no life to follow.

Does this world seem to be chaotic to you? Does your life seem to be filled with nothing but chaos? Now, I don't care where you want to begin with God . . . Old Testament or New Testament of the Bible. Wherever, you will find God at work through lots of seemingly unrelated events which, on a second look, allows us to peek in on God at work behind the scenes. Think of the preparation that had to take place to allow a little boy to be present on the hillside when it was lunch time. How did the five loaves and two fish get into his lunch basket at just the right time? Where did the fish pick up a coin in its mouth? And it was the exact amount needed to allow Jesus and Peter to pay their taxes! Think of the timing required to have a convoy of slave traders come just as Joseph's brothers were putting him into a pit. And as a result of this action, Joseph later would preserve a nation!

What about the North African who just happened to be in Jerusalem on one very special Friday, caught up with the mob, and finds himself carrying the cross of a man about to be crucified?! Yes, I know, you can smash all these incidents to bits and call them random happenings, just mere coincidence, another blip on the path of life. Consider with me the possibility that . . .

COINCIDENCE IS GOD AT WORK WISHING TO REMAIN ANONYMOUS!

Let's reverse our thinking and ask another question: Why do so many people fail in life? The bottom line to this question, pure and simple, is that people fail as a result of ignoring God and God's laws. Now you can come up with all kinds of other rationalizations . . . but think it through to the logical conclusion and eventually you might agree with my premise: People fail because they have ignored God or God's laws in their living and working. God wants to be included in your planning, living, and working. In short — if you are going to experience true success, God must be a part of it.

God has not made His rules for success deep, dark secrets. There are no secrets to success. The books written about success would fill many libraries, and now computer disks. But it seems as though each generation must re-discover these success truths for itself. Any book on success will tell you how, the steps to take, the goals to set, the plan to be created, and to keep on keeping on until it happens. Simple, profound, easy to read — but not as easy to do. But I am digressing . . . this is about finding that true success that allows you to experience it without guilt.

The Bible has a better word for success . . .

"PROSPER!"

Break it down in its Latin origin and you find "pro" meaning "for" and "sper" means "hope." Schaaazzam — you now have "according to your hopes"! Or "to prosper" means to "get what you hope for"! And no matter how you cut it, hope is one major ingredient in order to experience success of any kind.

Whatever it is that we hope for or work for, any success or prospering we do must not do any harm to anybody else. I know, there are all kinds of books and seminars teaching you how to swim with the sharks, how to be aggressive, how to be a power player, how to go for it and not worry about the people you have to step on or intimidate on your road to success.

Daddy Warbucks said this in the musical, "Annie:" "You don't have to be good to the people you meet on the way up if you don't plan to go down again."

In dealing with success from our perspective, it's not how much . . . but how you did it. If you are a biblical student, you have already noticed that there is a change in God's attitude in dealing with people. Early on, in Genesis, we discover that the main characters were people of great wealth . . . i.e., Abraham, Isaac, Jacob, Joseph, and so on. That doesn't count Adam, who owned all things but blew it.

However, there is a shift when we are introduced to a Saul and a David . . . nothings, nobodies in their nation, until God began to bless them. And then you can easily read about the condemnation heaped upon people who were rich. The biblical emphasis of such problems was not with the wealth but how people accumulated their wealth and used or abused others with it. There is a loud cry for equity and fairness and honesty in all business matters. When people abused this system, they were then condemned by God. For example, this has been preached at us by our forefathers:

> Now listen, you rich people, weep and wail because of the misery that is coming upon you. Your wealth has rotted, and moths have eaten your clothes. Your gold and silver are corroded. Their corrosion will testify against you and eat your flesh like fire. You have hoarded wealth in the last days. Look! The wages you failed to pay the workmen who mowed your field are crying out against you. The cries of the harvesters have reached the ears of the Lord Almighty. You have lived on earth in luxury and self-indulgence. You have fattened yourselves in the day of slaughter. You have

condemned and murdered innocent men,
who were not opposing you (James 5:1-6).

Powerful, harsh, condemnatory words! Yes . . . but
did you pick up the reasons for such condemnation? They
have hoarded it, failed to pay decent wages, lived in selfishness and self-indulgence, oppressed and condemned
others, and even have taken life away from others. There
are reasons for this strong language. The anger of the
writer, James, is leveled because some of the wealthy
were abusing others.

And because of such language . . . there has developed a strong "anti-wealth" philosophy which has been
preached and practiced for centuries. Even today, in our
enlightened day, there are good people who deny themselves any kind of success and deny for others the right
to experience any kind of success because of the fear
that it might lead to this kind of forbidden wealth and the
abuse of wealth. There are a lot of us who are struggling
with this mistaken belief out of the Puritan past. Again,
my friend, the Bible doesn't condemn or forbid success
or wealth. It does forbid the abuse and mis-use of others
that might be done with any accumulated wealth.

It's a recurring theme, this condemnation of wealth.
Let's read another passage out of the life of Daniel which
places what I am attempting to say into perspective:

> Therefore, O king, be pleased to ac-
> cept my advice: Renounce your sins by
> doing what is right, and your wickedness
> by being kind to the oppressed. It may be
> that then *your prosperity will continue* (Dan.
> 4:27, emphasis added).

Not all of us have been treated the same in life. And
we have all discovered that life is not fair. But God does
insist on the principle that all of us must treat others fairly,
honestly, and not abuse nor take advantage of anybody

in seeking our success. The wisest man who ever lived condensed it for us like this:

> Better a little with righteousness than
> much gain with injustice (Prov. 16:8).

This demand of God for fairness, honesty and non-abusive treatment is to cover all aspects of life — business dealings, money transactions, employment issues, purchases and sales — because all such dealings are to be based on the character and integrity of God. I strongly recommend that you read some of these God-given lifestyle concepts as well as business dealing precepts. An excellent place to start is with Leviticus 19. Let's just read two of these verses:

> Do not use dishonest standards when
> measuring length, weight or quantity. Use
> honest scales and honest weights, an hon-
> est ephah and an honest hin (Lev. 19:35-36).

Now comes the question, "WHY?" And we have that answer. It's found in a relationship that His people were to have with Him. They were to reflect the character of God in all their living, including all business dealings.

"I am the Lord your God" (Lev. 19:35).

These business/life principles become clear as a bell. When and if you use your wealth selfishly, abusing others, or misusing others . . . you can no longer count on heaven's help. You will suffer under the condemnation of God as well as others of His creation.

The late Mother Teresa of Calcutta was asked: "How do you measure the success of your work?"

She looked puzzled for a moment and then replied: "I don't remember that the Lord ever spoke of success. He spoke only of faithfulness in love. This is the only success that counts."

So how does this unselfish success really work out in real life. There are many illustrations which could be shared, but let's look in on a scene out of the sports world.

Perhaps you, along with millions, saw this unselfish attitude about success play out in the action at the 1984 winter Olympic games in Sarajevo, Yugoslavia. This story is told by Dennis Waitley in his book, *The Double Win*. The weather was anything but ideal for the men's slalom ski event. It was cold and bleak on Bjelasnica Mountain. A biting wind tore through the spectators gathered on this slope. This particular week of competition had been unpredictable.

The Mahre (pronounced Meyer) twins, Steve and Phil, were quiet and somber. This was to be their last competitive hurrah, their last battle with the world's finest skiers. Maybe they had won too often. They had just come off major wins in the World Cup competition. Now, an Olympic gold medal was maybe no big thing, according to the media. Their performance in the "giant slalom" event had been mediocre at best.

On this final day, Phil Mahre's number came up first. He wasn't real pleased with his first run, but the second run was a good, clean run. His combined time was 1 minute, 39:41 seconds — good enough to put him into first place. Still waiting at the top for his second run was twin brother Steve, whose good first run was leaving him with an excellent shot at the gold. Born only minutes apart and intense competitors, the Mahre twins were in their own private shoot-out for the Olympic gold!

The most "natural" thing for Phil to do was to wait, saying nothing, hoping his time would hold up against his twin brother's next run. Instead he grabbed a walkie-talkie and began radioing advice to Steve, who was still waiting at the top of the icy slope. Phil urged Steve to look ahead and ski a straight course, but he also warned that the bottom was icy slick.

Down came Steve who, by his own admission, made at least three mistakes that cost him valuable time. In addition, his skis got locked and he couldn't turn left properly on part of the run. With all that he still finished only .21 seconds behind his brother . . . good enough for a silver medal.

What about the walkie-talkie message? Steve said, "Phil has gold in his hand and he's telling me, 'Okay, you gotta do this to beat me.' "

Phil, in essence, said to his brother, "If I help you win, I win too! You may win today and I tomorrow, but I'm going to give you all my best, because that's what gives me the gold medal within!"

Phil and Steve hung up their competitive skis just after the Olympics in Sarajevo but they will always know what true, real success is:

> I will do my best and I will give my best. I will help fellow persons down the hill or up the hill, depending on their direction . . . all the while keeping my attitude and values in proper perspective. If I can in any way help you to succeed, I will also share in the victory. Therefore we both win! We both succeed! And together we have discovered that according to God . . . SUCCESS IS A TWO-WAY STREET![1]

> Blessed is the man who does not walk in the counsel of the wicked or stand in the way of sinners or sit in the seat of mockers. But his delight is in the law of the Lord, and on His law he meditates day and night. He is like a tree planted by streams of water, which yields its fruit in season and whose leaf does not wither. *Whatever he does prospers* (Ps. 1:1-3, emphasis added).

Chapter 1

True Success and the Mentoring Principle

Coming together is a beginning . . .
keeping together is progress . . .
working together is a success!

A "mentor" is a special kind of a person who fills the roles of being an advisor, counselor, preceptor, teacher, instructor, professor, tutor, monitor, proctor, master, guru, and guide. And we all are in need of such a person in our life. A mentor is one who has gone on before and has experienced some kind of success in life and is willing and able to help another achieve the same kind of success.

Sam Findley decided it was time to retire from the garment business which he had founded and built. So he called in his only son, Mervyn, and gave him the news along with this bit of advice: "Son, it's all yours! I've made a success of this business because of two principles . . . RELIABILITY and WISDOM. First, let's take reliability. If you promise goods by the tenth of the month, no matter what happens, you must deliver by the tenth. Even if it costs you overtime, double time, golden time. You always deliver what you promise!"

Mervyn thought about this and then asked, "But what about wisdom?"

His father shot back, "Wisdom is never making such a dumb promise!"

When you read the Bible, especially the Old Testament . . . you come to the realization that God, in His dealings with a number of people, made "covenants." A covenant is nothing more nor less than an agreement, a deal. If you do this, I will respond and do that. In today's language a "covenant" is a contract. And when we consider the setting of the biblical covenants that were made, these people made a deal with God. What an exciting concept!

The prime example of this deal-making took place at a mountain called "Sinai" and the man's name was Moses. This contract was written in stone — we call them the "Ten Commandments." (Notice, they were not the "Ten Suggestions.") But in addition to these ten commands . . . there was a whole lot more than these ten. You can read them, particularly in the Old Testament books of Leviticus and Deuteronomy. Lots and lots of . . . "If you do this and obey Me," then as your God "I will do such and such." Because of these covenants, or deals, God promised them a special land in which they were to live and also gave them the laws by which they were to live in the Promised Land. It's simple: if they obeyed and lived by the precepts as written, God would do his part. In this relationship, dependent upon conditions, then they would experience success! Here's how it was stated to them as they were about to enter into the Promised Land. This promise originally given to Moses was re-emphasized to Joshua:

> Be strong and very courageous. Be careful to obey all the law my servant Moses gave you; do not turn from it to the

right or to the left, that you may be *suc-cessful* wherever you go. Do not let this Book of the Law depart from your mouth; meditate on it day and night, so that you may be careful to do everything written in it. Then you will be prosperous and suc-cessful (Josh. 1:7-8, emphasis added).

Joshua became the successor to Moses! At the time of this renewing of a covenant, Joshua is approximately 85 years old and had been mentored by Moses for about 45 years. He had been the right-hand man, the second-fiddle, seasoned under the tutelage of a master. God had been the mentor to Moses, Moses passed leadership concepts, success concepts, along to his selected successor.

WHY IS GOD SO INTERESTED IN SUCCESSORS?

God has a very real task in dealing with human beings because He is eternal and we are finite. At longest, no human being lives very long. We have been promised 70 years . . . but what is this in comparison to eternity? So what good are long-term covenants, contracts, and deals with God if we can't live long enough to collect on them? One of God's solutions is for each of us to have a successor with whom God can continue the covenant. The other is to grant to us eternal life so that we can live with God forever to collect and enjoy the benefits of contracts made down here. How exciting! Here's one of the major arguments for heaven . . . it exists because God had to create it so all the terms of His contracts with finite humans could be fulfilled!

We can easily see this "successor-mentoring-replacement-duplicating" concept played out in the lives of the patriarchs . . . Abraham, Isaac, Jacob. Here it was father to son. But what God had promised to Abraham was not fulfilled until much later in the life of Joshua and his conquering of the land of Promise. Even here it wasn't completed because we, today, are still the recipients of the covenant made with Abraham and it will not be completed until we get to heaven! (See Gal. 3:6-9, 4:21-31; Rom. 4:1-25.) When God struck the covenant with Abraham, the language indicated His plan . . . not for Abraham only, but for all his descendants. "Know for certain that your *descendants*. . . . In the fourth generation your descendants. . . . To your descendants I give this land" (Gen. 15:13-18).

When a covenant was struck with Noah, notice the language: "I now establish my covenant with you *and with your descendants after you and with every living creature that was with you* (Gen. 9:9-10, emphasis added). But it didn't stop with this, God continued and brought it down to us, down to today: "And God said, 'This is the sign of the covenant I am making between me and you and every living creature, *a covenant for all generations to come*' " (Gen. 9:12, emphasis added). This principle is seen everywhere in the Bible: Abraham, Isaac, Jacob, Moses, Joshua, David, Solomon, and a whole succession of kings. Then there was Elijah, Elisha, Paul, and Timothy . . . to just name a few. Of course, Jesus Christ became the ultimate successor, and He even left someone to succeed Him — the Holy Spirit. In the broadest sense of meaning, the Church of today is the successor of Jesus Christ on this earth.

Notable, also, are the characters out of the Bible who left no successors behind. Joshua for example had no successors. Could that have been because his assignment was not completed? He did not drive out all the enemies and it was hundreds of years before Israel became strong enough again to control their land. Saul, the first king of Israel, did not leave any successors because he botched up the job so badly.

God took this principle so seriously that He was willing to disrupt entire nations in order to see this fulfilled. Look at the trouble He went to to ensure that Abraham and Sarah would have an heir, the successor to be the recipient of promises given to this elderly couple. Look at how the baby Moses was nurtured. The Nile River even complied in delivering this infant to the person of the princess. At the birth of Jesus Christ, Herod attempted to kill all the boy babies . . . escape was needed in order to preserve this ultimate successor.

This principle was so strongly stated and provisions made to continue that it was part of Jewish law. For example, a Jewish man was not successful until or unless he had a son to carry on in the next generation. In this law, if a man had a brother who had died childless, it became the duty of the surviving brother to father a child through the widow. Here's how it is stated in the biblical law: "The first son she bears shall carry on the name of the dead brother so that his name will not be blotted out from Israel" (Deut. 25:6).

Let's take another look at a familiar story and see this principle at work. David and Goliath are historical figures that all of us have studied or heard about. The name "Goliath" is not a Philistine name — this was a name apparently assigned to him by the Hebrews. It comes from a root Hebrew word "galah" which means to "denude" or "to make nude." So the literal meaning in Hebrew is that "Goliath is the one who takes captives and strips them naked." Can you think of a better definition of bondage? Goliath had intimidated and taken captive an entire army who cowered in fear. David arrives on the scene and to make a long story shorter, kills the giant, and in this action makes all of Israel free from this bondage and they all became heirs and successors because of his victory! God made a covenant promise to David that God would always provide an heir to the throne of David forever! This was fulfilled in the person of Jesus Christ, the

Son of David . . . a direct descendant of David, the one who became "the man after God's own heart."

```
TRUE BIBLICAL SUCCESS ALWAYS
      TAKES THE LONG VIEW!
```

Speaking of how this mentoring is to work, consider the story of Bob Kuechenberg, formerly a lineman with the Miami Dolphins. People go to college for all kinds of reasons but this one has to be unique. In an interview with Newsweek, Bob said: "My father and uncle were human cannonballs in carnivals. My father told me, 'Go to college or be a cannonball.' Then, one day my uncle came out of the cannon, missed the net, and hit the ferris wheel. I decided to go to college!"

Too often, in our cynical world, success of any kind is seen as a selfish accomplishment, a superman kind of a feat, a lonely entrepreneur against the world, a winner-take-it-all kind of an achievement. But this succession-mentoring principle calls all of us to a higher standard of success.

Any kind of biblical success did not stand alone. It is a link in the chain of history which is being forged. Success is real, true success when it also takes into account what will happen after the victory. Because of the single person victory of the boy shepherd David, the Philistine dynasty deteriorates. This is the turning point in making them a second-rate power. A single victory, yet an entire nation benefits! That's biblical success in every sense of the word. If this victory of David's were to stand alone it would be a fantastic feat of tumbling a giant. But think of the long-lasting, long-term benefits to a nation. This, too, was a major pivotal point in this nation's history. Think of how much more substantial this victory was when looked at from the perspective of a longer time line. It was a great short-term victory . . . but a much greater long-term success. Yes . . . I know that not every success of your life might have this kind of far-reaching effect. Yet, I believe that your successes are more far-reaching that you can ever imagine. They can all have eternal consequences.

> ### TRUE BIBLICAL SUCCESS ALWAYS LEAVES SOMETHING FOR OTHERS!

David's single-handed success also gave the inspiration to others of his people to experience their own victory. The account reads like this: "When the Philistines saw that their hero was dead, they turned and ran. Then the men of Israel and Judah surged forward with a shout and pursued the Philistines. . . . Their dead were strewn along the Shaaraim road" (1 Sam. 17:51-52).

Likewise, the victories that Joshua led his people to accomplish — crossing the Jordan River, defeating Jericho and Ai and more, allowed the people individually to also have their own personal victories. Especially Caleb, who when he was 85 years old said, "Now give me this hill country that the Lord promised me that day" (Josh. 14:12). The bottom line is this: "So Hebron has belonged to Caleb . . . ever since, because he followed the Lord" (Josh. 14:12-14).

This principle of sharing and leaving something for others was part and parcel of the law given to the nation. Here is the command, "When you reap the harvest of your land, do not reap to the very edges of your field or gather the gleanings of your harvest. Do not go over your vineyard a second time or pick up the grapes that have fallen. Leave them for the poor and the alien." Why? Here it is again, "I am the Lord your God" (Lev. 19:9-10). Every land owner was under this directive . . . leave something for tomorrow and for others who can also share in the bounty of a successful harvest!

> ## TRUE BIBLICAL SUCCESS MAY NOT BE REALIZED IN YOUR NAME OR IN YOUR LIFETIME!

The life of David provides us with so many principles by which to illustrate this concept. Just consider this: David, being the man after God's own heart, also had a vision to build a permanent house for God, a place where his people could worship — not a tent, not a temporary place of worship as it had been in his time. He was given credit for having the vision and he collected the money and materials with which to build this house of worship . . . but he was not allowed to build it. It was built during the lifetime of his successor, his son Solomon. David was given credit for the concept. Solomon fulfilled it in his time and built it in his name. David found this success and a successor when he was willing to step aside and let another benefit from his groundwork which flowed out of the success of his reign.

There's a part of the Bible which you probably have not spent much time reading — too bad. It's those overly long and booorrring genealogies. These have been written to show to us this principle at work in reality. "Abraham was the father of Isaac, Isaac the father of Jacob, Jacob the father of. . . ." The genealogy of Matthew concludes with "and Jacob the father of Joseph, the husband of Mary, of whom was born Jesus, who is called Christ"! Each of these previously mentioned people were successors . . . all leading up to the successor of all successors, Jesus Christ! There are some interesting people with some interesting stories of how they became a successor in the ultimate line of success. For example, there's the story of Rahab, a harlot, a prostitute who became part of this succession. Then there's Boaz, who married Ruth to keep alive the line of succession for another.

Do a bit of your own research to confirm into your spirit just how important this successor-mentor principle is to God! As these people found success, it was so that the succeeding generations could also find success. The abundance created by a successful person allowed the survival of the human race to continue in good and bad times. The success and abundance of the current generation allows the next to continue.

Some years ago, a young mother was making her way across the hills of South Wales, carrying her tiny baby in her arms. She was overtaken by a surprising, blinding blizzard. She soon lost her way and could no longer plow through the deepening snow. She never reached her destination and when the snowstorm had subsided, a search party found her beneath a mound of snow.

As they began to dig her out of the snow, they made an interesting discovery. Before she lay down in the snow, she had taken off her outer clothing and wrapped it around her baby. She had clutched her baby to her chest, lay down in the snow and used her body as a protection over her baby. She was dead . . . but to the great surprise and joy of her rescuers, the baby was alive and well. Once again, a mother had given her life for the life of her child, proving the depths of a mother's love. It was a success that blessed a successor, a survivor.

Oh, yes . . . here's the rest of that story: Years later, that child who survived was named David Lloyd George, who when grown to manhood, became prime minister of Great Britain! And according to historians, one of England's greatest statesmen!

Bible readers have created more wealth than any other people on earth, and have generated more happiness and hope than any people in history. Now, the new

generation must prepare to lead the re-
building of America! (Richard Gaylord
Briley)

Chapter 2

True Success and the Generosity Principle

Generosity doesn't make the world go round . . . but it sure makes the ride worthwhile!

This took place at the "Special Olympics" which were being held in Seattle, Washington. The participants had trained and worked and planned for these events for months. In fact, they may have worked harder than any athlete who had entered the regular Olympics. This particular event was the 100-yard-dash.

One young participant, at the sounding of the gun, leaped out in front of the others with the best start . . . however, each foot went in different directions and this well-meaning, well-trained athlete tripped and came tumbling down right in front of the starting blocks.

The other runners, each as eager as he was to compete in this event, stopped running and turned back to help their crying, fallen friend. In this heat, the crowd came to its feet as his competitors lovingly lifted him up and then all of them walked, linked arm in arm across the finish line together! These special Olympians had captured the true meaning of what Jesus and success are all about:

> ## NOBODY WINS UNTIL WE ALL WIN!

I wonder what kind of a world this would be if we all lived and played by this principle: That nobody wins until others do, TOO! If this really were in force . . . the people who have crossed the finish line first would be motivated to turn back to help others less able to also cross the finish line. Maybe you recall this saying out of your Sunday school days . . . "Jesus-Others-and-You, what a wonderful way to spell J-O-Y!" When true success is experienced, you will find that it is a "multiplier" and not a "divider." Real success is not selfish!

Take a moment and think this through with me. . . . Without a successful outcome, a success that generates a surplus, there could be no benevolence, no new jobs would be created, no way to make the church function, and no means to form a society. As long as we have the needy among us, we are in need of successful people who, from their surplus, can and will supply the necessities of life for others. When there is a surplus, there is also the possibility of giving which comes into play. When people experience success, others are blessed. If you were to eliminate the successful people among us, the roots that make possible the tree of civilization would soon dry up and wither away.

Here's one very important life principle that is always at work:

> ## EQUAL OPPORTUNITIES
> ## BUT UNEQUAL RETURNS!

Jesus illustrates this for us in one of His most well-known parables. Incidentally, Jesus told some 38 parables and most of them deal with money issues or success issues. Let's read it once more . . . but as though you have never read it before. Read it with fresh eyes and through a different set of glasses. Search for the success principle written above:

> A farmer went out to sow his seed. As he was scattering the seed, some fell along the path, and the birds came and ate it up. Some fell on rocky places, where it did not have much soil. It sprang up quickly, because the soil was shallow. But when the sun came up, the plants were scorched, and they withered because they had no root. Other seed fell among thorns, which grew up and choked the plants. Still other seed fell on good soil, where it produced a crop . . . a hundred, sixty or thirty times what was sown. He who has ears, let him hear (Matt. 13:3-9).

The math in this story breaks down quite easily: The birds ate 1/4 of the seed . . . another 1/4 was lost before it matured . . . then the weeds wiped out 1/4 . . . leaving only 1/4 to grow to maturity which produced a crop at harvest. But even in the harvesting . . . some of this productive 1/4 produced at different levels. Some produced a 30 times increase; some multiplied 60 times over; and the last portion multiplied 100 times. So, 1/3 of the productive 1/4 produced the majority of the harvest! And you see this law of "disproportionate returns" everywhere at work in our world.

We live in a world that was created by God to produce returns that are all out of proportion to the original investment. Consider the parable. Again, if you were to take one single kernel of good old American hybrid field corn and plant it, water it, fertilize it, and allow the sun, rain, and earth do their thing . . . what kind of a return can you expect? If you are an Iowa, Illinois, or Minnesota farmer you will get from a single kernel a single stalk of corn which produces two to three ears of corn per stalk. If you were to shuck that ear, you would discover approximately 720 kernels per ear! And when you are counting, you will discover that each ear always has an even number of rows and an even number of kernels. Talk about disproportionate returns! Why so much? So that there will be more than enough to survive and plant a crop for next year and the year after. The surplus allows the human race to continue. God is a generous God! A little can return a whole lot more! Where did the Microsoft Corporation start? With an idea in the head of Bill Gates. It wasn't full-blown to begin with, it started humbly, in a garage. It was starting small with a great idea. It's this kind of information which is stored in the DNA of the human soul.

God is generous and He expects that His sharing of generosity will also be a part of the living and lifestyle of people who have been blessed with a disproportionate return on their seed idea of the small idea, the small investment. Read it again and remember how this works:

> Do not judge, and you will not be judged. Do not condemn, and you will not be condemned. Forgive, and you will be forgiven. *Give, and it will be given to you.* A good measure, pressed down, shaken together and running over, will be poured into your lap. *For with the measure you use, it will be measured to you* (Luke 6:37-38, emphasis added).

Your generosity triggers the disproportionate returns.

When you give, you set into motion this law of reaping and sowing. And the thing to keep in mind is that you always reap more than you sow. That's why you plant seed, so that you can reap the harvest. The principle is everywhere in God's word. Consider:

> Do not be deceived: God cannot be mocked. A man reaps what he sows. The one who sows to please his sinful nature, from that nature will reap destruction; the one who sows to please the Spirit, from the Spirit will reap eternal life. *Let us not become weary in doing good, for at the proper time we will reap a harvest if we do not give up.* Therefore, as we have opportunity, let us do good to all people, especially those who belong to the family of believers (Gal. 6:7-10, emphasis added).

If God rewards and gives us more than we have sown and more than we deserve, that can be called the "grace" of God at work. If God gives us less judgment or evil than we deserve, that is called the "mercy" of God at work.

In an old order Amish community, a barn had been burned by an arsonist. The authorities finally found the arsonist. It turned out to be an Amish youth who, intent on rebellion, had set ablaze the barn of his Amish neighbor. When the press asked the farmer whose barn had been destroyed what punishment he thought the boy deserved, the man shook his head and with tears in his eyes, said, "It is we who have failed him somehow. I say 'Come home, son, and let's talk.' "

All their successful crops and farming techniques meant nothing if somehow their system had not given the young man all that he had needed. Again, nobody wins until others win, too.

QUESTION: IS IT POSSIBLE TO EXPERIENCE TRUE
SUCCESS WITHOUT GOD?

Sure! The answer is both "yes" and "no." And you know of lots of people who have achieved what would be termed as success in the eyes of this world. This they have won because becoming a financial success doesn't require miracles. Success is the result of a process and natural laws at work. It is possible to achieve monetary success, worldly acclaim, and fame without God. People have done it on their own. But if you were to track them and their work toward success, you would discover success principles at work.

One biblical story comes into play right here. It's one with which we are familiar. Jesus, again in His ministry, tells the story about the rich farmer who was called a "fool" by God. He obviously was prosperous because he might have been a good farmer, he may have had a good piece of land handed down to him by his own father, whatever, he was considered a success in the eyes of others. As you re-read this story . . . pick out the principle. His problem was not in having too much, not in having a bumper crop of produce, not in having too few barns, not in the wrong kind of planning. His failure came in his selfishness . . . he intended to hoard his crops for himself. Listen carefully as he speaks, "I'll say to myself, 'You have plenty of good things laid up for many years. Take life easy; eat, drink and be merry" (Luke 12:19). This is like saying there are no hurting, hungry, needy people in this world. There are no more orphans, no more widows, no more churches, no other empty barns, no empty cupboards anywhere around this area.

It's a theory of mine, no biblical backup . . . but I just happen to think that IF he had planned those bigger barns in order to warehouse some of that food for others, he would have survived that night! He didn't make it through the night. And it's a frightening bottom line of which Jesus speaks: "This is how it will be with anyone who stores up things for himself but is not rich toward God" (Luke 12:21). What a footnote! There is a point to be made here: Accountability is always a part of any personal success. Generosity with the surplus is important to God!

This brings up the question: How can we become rich towards God? If you were to read the rest of that chapter, the answer becomes obvious:

> But seek His kingdom, and these things
> will be given to you as well (Luke 12:31).

That is the key principle, spelled out for all time for all people, especially for people who are experiencing success of any kind. But it doesn't stop there, let's take it to the next level:

> Do not be afraid, little flock, *for your Father has been pleased to give you the kingdom.* Sell your possessions and give to the poor. Provide purses for yourselves that will not wear out, a treasure in heaven that will not be exhausted, where no thief comes near and no moth destroys. *For where your treasure is, there your heart will be also* (Luke 12:32-34, emphasis added).

Jesus dealt with this theme from many different angles. From His "Sermon on the Mount" we read: "So WHEN you give to the needy. . . ." It's not "if" . . . it's "WHEN." Expected, a command continued, "so that your giving may be in secret. Then your Father, who sees what is done in secret, will reward you" (Matthew 6:2-4).

We come back to the story of the rich farmer. . . . Jesus is not speaking against riches, per se, He is speaking not against the rich, but against those who love their riches too much. Probably the most telling rationalization of that rich farmer is this line, "I have no place to store my crops" or from another translation, "I have nowhere to bestow my goods."

Here's a personal observation of mine which has been based on some 38 years of pastoral ministry, which has covered about 1,976 weeks and an average of three church services a week in which there has been an offering taken. I have asked for, received, or observed more than 5,928 offerings in church. Thousands of dollars, in fact millions of dollars have been raised in this way. It has been most interesting to observe the process and observe people and their giving patterns over a long period of time. THE PEOPLE I HAVE FOUND OBSESSED WITH MONEY ARE RARELY THE WEALTHY! It's mostly the people who don't have a lot of money who have developed a ruthless belief that money, or at least enough of it, can supply all their needs. They lack experience with money. "Christians" who have refused to give and be generous with their means and stewardship practices are pygmy Christians in other areas of their lives also.

Anonymous givers are fascinating. And sometimes shocking! Maybe you remember an article about a very generous man, which appeared in *Time* magazine, February 3, 1997. The man's name is Charles Feeney. He's the man who made his fortune by owning and developing the concept of those "duty-free" shops you see in airports, seaports, and aboard cruise ships. Secretly he has been giving his fortune away. The only reason we know who he is and what he has done is because in the selling of his business he was facing a lawsuit which required him to divulge all the giving he had done. Feeney has been like the most deep-pocketed Santa you can imagine.

Just how much has he given away? The incredible sum of $600 MILLION over the past 15 years! That's not all, he has stuck away an addition 3 1/2 BILLION into his two charitable foundations so it can be given away later!

And still he is not poor! He kept $5 million for himself . . . about 1/10th of one percent of what he has given away!

Why? What motivates a man to give out of his surplus like that? Incidentally, he does not own a car or a house. He told the *New York Times,* "I simply decided I had enough money."

Now this is a rich man! Not because he is a multi-millionaire, not because he has given away millions, but because he has decided, "I have enough."

What a "secret" of success! But Charles Feeney is behind the times in implementing this philosophy of living. An obscure man by the name of Agur has penned a prayer for all of us in regards to finding balance in our success:

> Two things I ask of you, O Lord; do not refuse me before I die: Keep falsehood and lies far from me; *give me neither poverty nor riches, but give me only my daily bread.* Otherwise, I may have too much and disown you and say "Who is the Lord?" Or I may become poor and steal, and so dishonor the name of my God (Prov. 30:7-9, emphasis added).

True success can be yours when you have learned the principle that lives in a generous spirit of giving and sharing the fruits of success with others. At what level of giving should be the minimum? Have you heard of the "tithing" principle? It's the giving of the first 10 percent of all your earnings or the increase of your investments. Where did that come from? That's God's plan which was instituted from almost the very beginning of His dealings with mankind. The record tells us that "Melchizedek . . . met Abraham returning from the defeat of the kings and blessed him, and *Abraham gave him a tenth of everything*" he had gathered as he plundered these enemies.

(Gen. 14:17-20). The success of Abraham was shared with Melchizedek, who was a forerunner of Jesus Christ who was to come later. We start with this tenth by giving it to the church at which we worship.

Do you really want to open the windows of blessing to be poured out upon you? Here's the secret as written by the prophet:

> "Bring the whole tithe into the store-house, that there may be food in my house. Test me in this," says the Lord Almighty, "and see if I will not throw open the flood-gates of heaven and pour out so much blessing that you will not have room enough for it. I will prevent pests from de-vouring your crops, and the vines in your field will not cast their fruit [prematurely]" says the Lord Almighty. "Then all nations will call you blessed, for yours will be a de-lightful land," says the Lord Almighty (Mal. 3:10-12).

And here's the rub, here's the test: it's a money is-sue and it is a generosity issue.

If you want to truly experience all the success which is possible . . . it starts with an act of generosity, giving.

Sadhu Singh, who is an Indian Christian, and a friend were traveling across a pass high up in the Himalayan Mountains. At one point they happened upon a body lying in the snow on the trail. Sundar wished to stop and help the nearly frozen man, but his traveling companion refused, saying, "We shall lose our lives if we burden ourselves with him in this snowstorm."

But Sundar refused to think of leaving the man to die in the ice and snow. As his traveling companion told him farewell, Sundar lifted the poor traveler and carried him over his shoulders on his back. With great exertion on his part, he carried the man. Gradually, the heat from Sundar's body began to warm the poor frozen fellow and he came to, revived. Soon both were walking together side by side. Then, they caught up with Sundar's former companion . . . frozen to death in the below-zero freezing cold and wind.

In this case . . . Sundar Singh was willing to lose his life on behalf of another . . . and in this process really found it, while his callused, selfish companion attempted to save his own life only to lose it!

Success in your life is God's way of blessing others through you, while you benefit yourself. Some of the most dangerous people in the world are those who are self-made, who worship the creator called "self," who are always looking out for #1.

Here's a story which captures the essence of the "generosity" principle in success. At the International Youth Triennium in Bloomington, Indiana, in July 1980, Professor Bruce Riggins of McCormick Theological Seminary was speaking to some 3,800 young people. In his presentation he told of meeting a dedicated Christian lady working in an amazing way with the under-privileged people of London, England. He was interested in what had inspired her personal Christian faith and action.

In answer to his question, she told her story. She was a Jewess fleeing from the German Gestapo in France during World War II. She knew she was close to being caught and she had wanted to give herself up. She came to the home of a French Huguenot. Another widow lady came to that home to say that it was time to flee to another hiding place. This Jewish lady said, "It's no use, they will find me anyway. They are so close behind."

The Christian widow then said, "Yes, they will find someone here, but it's time for you to leave. Go with these people to safety. . . . I will take your identification and wait here."

This Jewish lady then understood the plan. The Gestapo would come and find this Christian widow and take her for the fleeing Jewess.

As the professor listened to this story, the now-Christian lady of Jewish descent looked him in the eye and said: "I asked her why she was doing that and the widow responded, 'It's the least I can do; Christ has already done that and more for me.' "

The widow was captured and imprisoned in the Jewish lady's place, allowing her to successfully make her escape. Inside of six months the Christian widow was dead in the concentration camp into which she was placed.

Real, true success looks like this: JESUS — OTHERS — YOU! WHICH IS ANOTHER WAY TO SPELL: JOY!

NOBODY WINS UNTIL WE ALL WIN!

Chapter 3

True Success and the Consent Principle

*The secret of success lies not in doing
what you like to do but in giving yourself
permission to succeed!*

Christian Herter, while serving as governor of Massachusetts, was running for re-election. One day, after a very early start and an equally busy morning with no lunch, followed by an afternoon equally packed, he arrived at a church barbecue in the late afternoon. Herter was famished. As the Governor moved down the serving line, he held out his plate to the lady serving the barbecued chicken. She put one piece on his plate and turned to the next person in line. "Excuse me," Governor Herter said, "do you mind if I have another piece of chicken?"

"Sorry," said the lady, "I'm only supposed to give one piece to each person."

"But, I'm starved," replied the governor.

"Sorry, move along," the lady resolutely replied.

The governor was a modest man, but he was also famished and decided that he could throw his weight around just a bit. "Lady, do you know who I am?" he said. "I'm the governor of Massachusetts."

The lady replied, "Do you know who I am? I'm the lady in charge of the chicken. Now, move along, mister!"

She had given herself approval to succeed at her assigned task! To give yourself "consent" is to . . . agree, concur, assent, approve, accept, accede, acquiesce, submit, permit, allow, sanction, confirm, ratify, and endorse which is the action thinking of consent. The noun side of granting "consent" is to give agreement, authorization, the right, license, confirmation, sanction, accord, and permission. Quite a concept, but how many of us have really given ourselves this kind of a go-ahead in the pursuit of success?

When you get down to the very bottom line, all success is a voluntary process. But we can also flip the coin over and say that failure is also voluntary. It's a matter of choice. We tend to move or live in the direction toward the one aspect of which we have given the most consent, regardless of what we or others may say or think. In order for any kind of success to take place in your life and living, you must consent to it! You must give yourself permission to succeed! Of all the concepts we are looking at in this book, this may be the least understood. Not everybody has given themselves this inner "consent," this inner acceptance, this inner confirmation to move in the direction of any attempts at finding success. This holds true for many Christians, too. There is something deep in our souls which cannot give full release so the pursuit of success can take place.

If you listen carefully to some people as they talk, you hear this expressed in many ways: "Everything seems to be against me," or "I guess I'm a born loser," or "Look at me, I'm just a failure," or "Nothing in life seems to work for me." Could it be that such people have never granted themselves acceptance enough so that they can make an effort at success? Could it be that some have had their "permission" stolen away by circumstances or wrong teachings or abusive people?

One of the most powerful statements granting approval or consent was spoken by a writer named John:

> To all who received Him, to those who believed in His name, *He gave the right to become children of God* (John 1:12).

Powerful! Consent is an event, statement, ritual, or happening that grants to you the authority to change your life or to change your behavior! In this case, it's a promise of God, a gift of God given to you, which you can also give to yourself. If God said it, then it's believable, then I can take it for me! Think of the immense possibilities provided here — the right to become a child of God! Incredible! The implications of this promise are almost beyond belief!

When David won his battle with the giant Goliath, it granted permission to all his Israelite brothers to also fight and live and act like victors! You remember the story of how they poured out of their hilltop position and pursued the Philistines, killing them, destroying them, plundering them, because David had won and thereby gave to all of them the right to also do the same thing. If there is a hidden "secret" of success, this may come the closest to being it. Not too many books, seminars, or success speakers ever talk about this concept. It's an obscure concept, overlooked, and not given much thought. But think about it with me and you might discover that this is the principle which has not allowed you to be the success you think you should be. Have you given yourself the inner release, really granted to yourself the right to be a success?

The resurrection of Jesus Christ from the dead was this kind of giving a consent to others to live differently.

Before His resurrection, nobody had the audacity or permission or authority to say, "Silver or gold I do not have, but what I have I give you. In the name of Jesus Christ of Nazareth, walk" (Acts 3:6). The story which follows this event is wonderful when you consider how these two men expressed their faith. Their lifestyle was now so changed, so different, that the leaders of the day couldn't believe what they were hearing and observing. Their response? "When they saw the courage of Peter and John and realized that they were unschooled, ordinary men, they were astonished and they took note that these men had been with Jesus" (Acts 4:13).

What changed Peter and John and all the other Apostles? The words and now the resurrection of Jesus! By His words and His miraculous resurrection, consent had been granted for these men to now act differently! This consent is a basic human need and desire. How many people have gone through life seeking for approval for their success from a parent who has refused to give it? How many are struggling inside because this permission from a parent was never given before death took them away? We have been raised by the permission parents have given to us for the first 18 or so years of living. Without their permission we weren't permitted to do anything. Without the granting of consent or approval, we keep locked up inside of us all the talents and gifts and desires. We are defeated before we even get started in life. Now, when we are adults, it is a constant groping for someone to give us the approval we so desperately need. But most importantly of all, we must give ourselves the approval to go for it.

WHY DO OTHERS PROSPER WHO ARE WICKED AND WE DON'T?

Lots of thinking minds have wrestled with that question. The clue may be in the concept we are considering.

The wicked, the heathen, the infidel, when they come up with a dream, don't have to struggle with the getting of consent or approval . . . they just go for it. But when we are Christians, we struggle with the ethics of it, the wrongful teachings we have heard, the wrong thinking that success is bad, and therefore must jump through all kinds of spiritual hoops before we can finally feel comfortable enough with success to go after it. The wicked act, then think. They require much less mental gymnastics when they see an opportunity. One reason for people not succeeding is lack of effort. For the wicked, they jump on each new opportunity as it is presented while we are left at the gate, still floundering around for permission to proceed. We look at the Bible, we hopefully look to others, we seek out our parents, we run it by friends, we procrastinate until the opportunity is lost. We're left at the gate, still attempting to get out of the garage, and by the time we have done all we feel we must do before we can pursue the opportunity, it's too late.

> ## REAL SUCCESS REQUIRES MORE THAN HARD WORK AND OBEDIENCE!

Without this inner release, true success is impossible and it is highly unlikely that success can ever be attained. Have you ever noticed that the people who feel guilty about success are always apologizing for what little they might have achieved? You will experience no more success than you have given yourself the approval to achieve. This is the inner authority to do and continue the life actions which will lead ultimately to success. The prophet has captured the essence of what I have been attempting to say:

If you are *willing and obedient*, you will

eat the best from the land; But if you resist
and rebel, you will be devoured. . . . For
the mouth of the Lord has spoken (Isa.
1:19-20).

Willing AND obedient . . . two ingredients. Either
one is not enough, these two go together. Obedience
has to do with what we are commanded to do. Willingness applies to what we want to do. Too many people
get all hung up and hung out on the obedience part and
never get to the willing, the consent part of what God
has set in motion. God expects something called initiative on your part. Are you willing? That's half. Are you
obedient? That's the other half in this pursuit of success.
There are a whole lot of things God expects us to do
without being told! If we don't do the good that we know
we ought to be doing, there are penalties. Initiative is
doing without being told! Is that biblical? Yes! For start-
ers, read again the parable which Jesus told late in His
earthly ministry about the talents. Five, two, and one,
given to three men. Two of these used initiative, WITH-
OUT BEING TOLD, and invested their talents to produce
more. But what of the one-talented man? He hid his talent, he buried it in the ground where it did nobody any
good. It didn't even collect interest. The least he could
have done, so said Jesus, was to have placed it with an
investment banker, without being told! There was an ex-
pectation of results from the Master. Obedience applies
to what we are told to do, willingness applies to what
we want to do and what we should be doing!

During the Tonkin Gulf crisis, a few years ago, Henry
Kissinger asked an assistant to prepare an analysis. The
assistant worked night and day for a week and put the
document on Mr. Kissinger's desk only to receive it back
within the hour. Affixed to the report was a note asking
that it be re-done. The assistant dutifully redid it; he had
slept only nine hours for the entire week. The document

again went on Mr. Kissinger's desk; an hour later it was returned with a note from Kissinger asserting that he expected better and asked that the work be done again. So the assistant went back to the drawing board again. Another week of intense work and then the assistant asked if he might present it personally to Mr. Kissinger. When he came face to face with Henry Kissinger, he said, "Mr. Kissinger, I've spent another sleepless week. This is the very best I can do."

Said Mr. Kissinger: "In that case, now I'll read it."

> ### CONSENT IS A POWERFUL TOOL TO BE USED FOR ACHIEVING SUCCESS!

Why do people fail? Lots of reasons can be seen. But what about those failures that seem to have no plausible explanation? How about the people who seem to be experiencing success and all of a sudden have a disaster strike? How is it that brilliant people can do stupid things which cause failure? This can be called "the unconscious need to fail."

Was there anybody in the world who had a chance against the World's Heavyweight Champion, Joe Louis? In 1941 fight promoters, sportswriters, and boxing fans scoured the bushes for at least one credible heavyweight contender.

Billy Conn, a stylish Irish boxer from Pittsburgh, had risen through the ranks by speed and cleverness. He was not a terrific puncher, only 12 of his 58 wins were by knockout. He had footwork, canniness, and command of the ring. Most agreed he was one of the smartest boxers to step into the ring . . . but not smart enough! The fight took place on June 18, 1941, at the Polo Grounds in New York. As a crowd of 55,000 sat dumbfounded, Conn took command of the fight. His plan worked. Conn was win-

ning the fight . . . by the 13th round he had a command-
ing lead. He laughed at the befuddled Joe Lewis. This
was the biggest upset in the fight game. Then . . . the
fight changed, Billy Conn began throwing harder punches.
Conn was then attempting to knock out Lewis. Conn
waded in, but left one momentary opening! Lewis connected with a right hand and Conn was counted out with
just two seconds to go in the 13th round.

Afterwards, Conn said that he was beating Joe Lewis
so badly that he decided to knock Lewis out. Then he
commented that he probably didn't deserve to be the
heavyweight champ of the world. His strategy worked
so well that he abandoned it to adopt the ONLY tactic
that gave Lewis a chance to win the fight.

This is in reality a reverse expression of pride. Success can be a burden, winning can become a pain. Why?
Because successful people must keep on being a success! Winners must keep on winning! So we and others
think. Without that inner quality of consent, we can always find a way to conveniently lose.

> It is important to understand what fail-
> ure is . . . and what it isn't. Success and
> failure are not polar opposites, they are
> parts of a continuum. One can lead to the
> other with great ease. Neither is likely to
> be permanent; the irony is we believe both
> will last forever. (Carol Hyatt and Linda
> Gottlieb)

One method of insuring failure is to organize the
opposition. The logic behind such destructive thinking
seems to be that without the inner consent to be a winner, once you defeat an opponent, make sure he remains
an opponent. On a mega-scale, this has been played out
for all to see. The winners of World War I, most notably
France, ground Germany into the dust with the Versailles

Treaty, making it possible for Hitler to rise to power and divert the course of history down an even more bloody and tragic path. The person who doesn't have that inner release to pursue success is one who can consistently set it up in such a way so efforts at being a success will be sabotaged by enemies which have been created.

Ben Hecht wrote: "The wise man knows that he has only one enemy: HIMSELF! This is an enemy difficult to ignore and full of cunning. It's an enemy never to be forgotten."

We must start to look within. What do you see? What do others see? What does God see inside of your soul? Who is that person mirrored in your soul? What is holding you back from being the success you want to be? Children don't seem to have this problem . . . unless some adult has stolen from them that precious element called consent.

A husband and wife were driving along a busy city street, searching for a parking place. They spotted one and pulled in. There on the sidewalk, was a stocky five or six-year-old boy standing with arms folded, erect, rigid. "You can't park here!" he yelled at them.

"Why not?"

"Because," he announced to them and to the world, "I am a fire hydrant!"

No problem there with consent! Maturity is accepting responsibility for ourselves. Maturity is the capacity to make constructive use of our innermost thoughts. To be mature is to advance toward maturity. The practical life test is not what we are now . . . but where we are going. Everybody needs values, not something abstract. This "value system" is the control device that guides behavior in all circumstances.

How can this inner voice be changed? One step is to become accountable to the concepts which we read from the Word of God. We must become accountable to the person and presence of Jesus Christ. We must become accountable to others around us . . . spouse, family, friends, and church. Allow some of these relationships to mature to the place where others can ask some of those "white-knuckle" kinds of questions. Have you given yourself consent to do the actions and keep doing those things which have the possibility of leading you to success in your life, in your career, in your home, in your church, in your community?

Without this inner consent, virtually all progress stops. This world system runs on rituals of granting consent. Think of some of these with me. Graduations, which begin as soon as pre-school, are all rituals of passage, the right to be and continue. A wedding grants to two people the permission to become husband and wife and to parent a family. A swearing-in oath given to a man allows him to serve as a judge. When a person wears a special uniform it grants the rights and privileges to act as a policeman, soldier, sailor, referee. Without a uniform, football players would look pretty dumb going out for a pass or tackling another person. When such events are presided over by authority figures there is permission granted. You see it in the Bible when the father blessed his eldest son. David was anointed to be a king by Samuel the prophet so that David could begin doing the things a king is supposed to do. When Peter stood up on the Day of Pentecost to preach his dynamic sermon, he had permission granted to him by the resurrection power of Jesus Christ as well as the ritual of being filled with the Holy Spirit.

We could go on and on. . . . The Declaration of Independence has granted to lots of people the right to pursue success and happiness in building a new nation. We have been granted approval to go after life, liberty, and happiness. Without a doubt, next to the Bible, this document crafted and signed on July 4, 1776, has been the most powerful permission-granting instrument ever devised in the world's history. Such approval, when it has been internalized, can change your life and your future. Folks, the sooner we grant to ourselves this inner approval for living, the sooner we become mature people, the sooner we find our success in life, the sooner we find that fulfillment, and enjoy the happiness which arises out of a productive lifestyle. Without this ritual, without this wholehearted inner approval, we will remain stuck in a do nothing, attempt nothing, succeed at nothing syndrome.

I remind you that success is not the result of a miracle! True success is the result of making the right choices, performing the right actions, and instilling the right disciplines. Success is a system which anyone can learn. It is not a deep dark secret for only the chosen few! Consent is yours by giving it to yourself! You have permission to grant it to yourself so you can make the right decisions, perform the needed actions, and think correctly. YOU can be a success! YOU have the right to give yourself inner approval! YOU are special! YOU have been created by the Creator of successful principles to also be successful!

When Dawson Trotman passed away, he probably left behind a legacy of discipleship and success rarely matched on this earth. He died in Schroon Lake, New York. He died in the middle of an area that he was an expert in . . . he drowned! He was an expert swimmer. The last few moments of life that he had in the water were spent in rescuing one girl out of the lake. He dove back down into the depths of that lake to retrieve and rescue the other girl. He lifted her to the surface and then submerged again and was not found until a dragnet found him some few hours later.

A man named Larson was on the boat when Trotman died and he said: "The entire United States Navy couldn't have saved Trotman that day . . . it was God's time."

Time magazine ran an article on Trotman's life the next week and they captioned it: "Always Holding Somebody Up." In one sentence they captured Trotman's life . . . his investment in people, honesty, humility, and success in his ministry. Always holding others up.

That's success, any way you want to measure it!

Chapter 4

True Success and the Reliability Principle

*You become successful the moment you
start moving toward a worthwhile goal
and keep on moving day in and day out!*

Bernie and Elaine Lofchick of Winnipeg, Canada, are the parents of David, born with cerebral palsy. Thirty doctors said there was no hope for their son and advised them to put him in an institution for his own good and for the good of the normal members of the family.

The Lofchicks, however, when David was two, finally found a doctor who was oriented toward solutions, not problems. He was the world-famous Dr. Pearlstein from Chicago. Bernie was able to get an appointment when a little boy from Australia canceled his, and they went to Chicago for the examination, which was very comprehensive. Dr. Pearlstein spelled out what would be required if they expected David to make the progress he knew David could make.

One of the things was consistency in treatment. Every single day, every time. One item illustrates . . . they were to put heavy braces on his legs, and every night they were to be tightened. Consequently the pain constantly increased for David. Many, many times he protested because of the pain. David was a cute little boy: coal black hair, olive complexion, beautiful green eyes. With tears he would plead, "Mom, do you have to put them on tonight?" But his parents loved David so much they said "no" to the tears of the moment so they could say "yes" to the joy and laughter of a lifetime which was to follow. There were daily exercises, daily regimens to keep, therapy, and much more. They were not to skip a single one because if they missed, David would experience a setback. Consistency and reliability were the disciplines of each day.

Today "Little David" is an adult. . . . He weighs in at 195 pounds, has a barrel chest and is the #1 condominium salesman with the #1 real estate firm in Winnipeg, Canada. He is one outstanding young man in every way. Through faithfulness and reliability, Bernie and Elaine, along with David, overcame the problems in order to experience success![2]

No matter how you might like to slice it, the fact is that today more people are alive, well-fed, adequately housed, and better educated than at any other time in human history. Who deserves the credit? Largely the people who have been readers of the most outstanding book on success ever written, the Bible. These people have found the keys to life-changing ideas and concepts which, when followed, have led to new successes while others are still looking for the keys that will unlock success for them.

Reliability is a term which is easier to define than it is to live out. The term "reliable" can be better understood in other words like these: dependable, faithful, trustworthy, trusty, responsible, solid, sound, conscientious, tried and true. One of life's goals is to become a reliable person. Someone to be counted on, someone who can be trusted to show up time after time. This is a bedrock type of character issue. Do you live by faith? Are you faithful? How important are these life issues to success? Without them there will be no real success.

> Now faith is being sure of what we
> hope for and certain of what we do not see.
> This is what the ancients were commended
> for (Heb. 11:1-2).

That is a powerful statement . . . but, really, how important is faith to success, and to all of living, for that matter? Read the following statement carefully because it brings into focus the importance that God places in these concepts.

> Without faith it is impossible to please
> God, because anyone who comes to him
> must believe that he exists and that he re-
> wards those who earnestly seek him (Heb.
> 11:6).

Now that is one incredible statement! Impossible to please God without it! That makes it an absolute requirement for all of us to cultivate. How much faith is necessary to please God? Simply, do you believe that He exists? Yes or no? And the second requirement is: Do you believe that He rewards people who earnestly seek Him? Yes or no? Simple, to the point, easily understood. Faith is not something way off beyond our comprehension. It's right here on the first-floor level. Two requirements: believe He exists and that He rewards people who earnestly pursue after Him. Faithfulness and reliability grow out of this bedrock foundation built on faith. What happens when people lose their faith and consequently their faithfulness?

If you don't believe that God exists . . . why go any farther? That is the end of this exercise. If you believe that God exists, then you also believe in what He has said to you from His Word. The concepts of success to which we are looking for insight and direction are from the Person of God. These are His concepts, these are His principles, these are His directives. If we believe He exists . . . we also believe that there are rewards for following His direction. If we do it His way we, too, can experience success without guilt!

Do you know how the great composer Tchaikovsky died? There is more than one version to this story . . . but according to one, perhaps the most reliable source, the end of Tchaikovsky's life was determined four days after one of his symphonies received an unfavorable reception in St. Petersburg. He then told his friends that he had lost his faith so that life wasn't worth living anymore. The great composer, despondent, deliberately drank a glass of unboiled water in the middle of a cholera epidemic. His friends who witnessed this were appalled. Tchaikovsky told them he had lost his faith and that he was less afraid of cholera than other illnesses. Cholera, however, didn't share his opinion and it soon finished him off. Why? A faith that is lost can kill you. Living without hope can kill you.

> ## FAITH IS A FUNCTION OF TIME
> ## AND NOT OF ETERNITY!

Faith works in this life . . . however, when time shall be no more, neither shall faith be needed. The rewards for living by faith and faithfulness with reliability are found out of this life — heaven is the ultimate reward for such people. But there are rewards for living by faith and exercising faithfulness here and now in this life. Success is the reward for those who have believed in it and pursued after it with consistency. The kind of faith I'm talking about is not a passive, intellectual kind of mental assent. The faith that works is a faith that sweats! Faith works hard. There is the belief which is followed by the action. The Bible tells us that if you have only faith you are only halfway to the goal. Faith, in order to be faith, must be mixed with actions. Just like two oars in the same boat. If you used only one oar, you'd go in circles, but with two of them pulling together, you can make progress.

In the Bible, people of faith were praised for their faithfulness, their reliability, their consistency. Sometimes, all you have to do to become a winner is to show up every day. The people who are cited for their faith were persistent, steady, stable, consistent kinds of people. It's a discipline which can be learned. Faith is translated into faithfulness when you are ready to act upon your beliefs.

> "Have faith in God," Jesus answered. "I tell you the truth, if anyone says to this mountain, 'Go throw yourself into the sea,' and does not doubt in his heart but believes that what he says will happen, it will be done for him. Therefore, I tell you, whatever you ask for in prayer, believe that you have received it, and it will be yours" (Mark 11:22-24).

The problem may not be with our belief system. It may be with our lack of action which follows. If we really believed, we would act upon it. There is a story about a woman who had been subject to hemorrhaging for 12 years and all her efforts and different doctors had amounted to nothing. In fact, she was broke and worse off than before. But she believed that if she could simply touch the Master's cloak, that she would be healed. Suppose that she had only believed and done nothing about it? How would she have ever touched His garments? What if she had stayed at home, believing it could happen and making no effort to press through the crowds until she had accomplished her pursuit? Her action made her belief a reality. It would have been easy to have given up — the crowds were huge and tightly packed. She may have had to make an arduous journey to even get to where the crowds were. The day may have been hot, she may have been thirsty and hungry, but still she pressed on because her faith kept her actions alive. Success of any kind will not happen only because you believe, you must also act!

Faith is the belief that someday, at some time, at some place, success will happen if it is pursued faithfully. Faith combined with faithfulness will have a synergistic effect on your life and your living.

One year, at the Iowa State Fair, an old-fashioned horse pulling contest was to be held. In this event a sled or skid is pulled along the ground with more and more weight added every 50 feet or so until the horse or team can no longer move the sled. The grand champion draft horse pulled a sled with some 4,500 pounds loaded on it. The runner-up pulled some 4,400 pounds. Some of the farmers wondered what they could pull if hitched together. Separately, they had totaled 8,900 pounds. When hitched together and pulling as a team, they pulled a total of 12,500 pounds!

> ## DEPENDABILITY HAS A MUCH BETTER MARKET VALUE THAN CLEVERNESS!

You likely will never know how many people will be touched and how far-reaching it can be when you believe and then live it out consistently, day in and day out. When you express your faith with reliability, it goes far beyond simple monetary success.

How about a simple personal example for you to

consider. Can you save at least $1,000 per year? That's $83.33 per month. A bit less than $20 per week figured over 52 weeks. Could you also begin this plan at age 30 and continue doing it until you attain age 65? Can you faithfully commit to carry this out? If you consistently follow this plan and do not touch your seed money and pay your taxes from another source of income, and if you invest this amount to receive an average of 15 percent compounded interest . . . at age 65 you will have accumulated approximately $1,000,300! That's how easy it is to become a millionaire! If you believe this and this is one of your goals . . . with consistency you can attain it!

But we are Americans and Americans are funny people! We want "instant" everything to happen for us! Who has the patience and commitment to continue until the goal is reached? We are willing to give generously to find cures for all kinds of diseases . . . but are not willing to spend any time, money, or effort on preventing disease. We want to lose weight by taking a pill instead of consistently practicing discipline. We want to experience exciting success without putting any effort into it. We want to make heaven our eternal home . . . but would just as soon not pay the price in the present. Oh, yes, we want to go to heaven eventually.

In looking at "success" in the broadest sense of the word . . . not too many people are willing to pay the price on a consistent basis, with reliability, and keeping with the plan. There are no shortcuts to success. It takes hard work. The only place where success appears before work is in the dictionary. To become a reliable person is to understand that there are not any easy-success-pills to swallow.

> Now . . . it is required that those who
> have been given a trust must prove faithful
> (1 Cor. 4:2).

It's been said that without a purpose we exist in a world of non-specifics. When daily activity is governed by hit-and-miss actions we become dependent on whatever comes our way. Consider the drifter on the street approached by a streetwise social worker:

Social Worker: "Where do you live?"
Drifter: "Here and there."
Social Worker: "What do you eat?"
Drifter: "This and that."
Social Worker: "What do you do for a living?"
Drifter: "Anything and everything."
Social Worker: "When do you bathe?"
Drifter: "Now and then."
Social Worker: "You should sign up for government assistance."
Drifter: "When would I get it?"
Social Worker: "Sooner or later."

Contrast the above with the following, which gives "mad" a whole new meaning. On May 3, 1980, Cari Lightner's life was ended by a drunken driver. This tragic event changed the course and focus of her mother's life.

In the midst of the sorrow and stress of losing a child, Candy Lightner made a vow not to let this tragedy and others like it go unnoticed. Only four days after her daughter's death, Candy met with other friends to discuss what they could do to make an impact on drunken-driving fatalities. Her life took on a whole new meaning that day as "Mothers Against Drunk Driving" (MADD) was born.

This handful of purpose-driven ladies grew to 20 as they demonstrated in California's capital, Sacramento. Then they went on to Washington, D.C., where 100 people marched in front of the White House. They were committed to reducing drunk-driving disasters. Someone had to listen! They kept at it.

The consistent efforts of this core group ultimately resulted in over 360 chapters throughout the world, a national commission against drunk driving, and more than 400 new laws in 50 states addressing drunk driving. In addition, young people concerned about losing friends formed "Students Against Drunk Driving" (SADD).

Amid the tears, cheers, and jeers, Candy Lightner believed that people who cared enough about their purpose could have an impact on the world around them. And she is right! Candy turned personal disaster into monumental achievement by setting her course and following it day after day!

WHAT WOULD YOU BE DOING IF YOU KNEW YOU HAD ONLY SIX MORE MONTHS TO LIVE?

Really, who says you have six months more? What will you be doing NOW, today, to reach your goals, to attain your success, to make this a better place in which to live?

Martin Luther King, Jr. exclaimed: "Even if I knew the world would end tomorrow, I would plant a tree today."

Saint Augustine said, "I would continue hoeing my garden."

These were two men who were committed to their purpose, sticking consistently with their plan, and time or the lack of it, would not change their course.

Make the contrast of these two with the Russian novelist Leo Tolstoy, who possessed what many would have considered the best in life. He was in his mid-forties, healthy, rich, famous, and happily married, and had stated that these outward signs of success were not indicators of inner fulfillment. He wrote: "A strange condition of mental terror began to grow upon me. . . . The same questions continually presented themselves to me: 'Why?' and 'What afterward?' My life had come to a sudden stop. I could breathe, eat, drink, sleep . . . indeed I couldn't help doing so. But there was no real life in me. . . . Life had no meaning for me."

There is a line from the movie, "Joe Versus the Volcano" which may fit here. Told that he had six months to live, Joe marched up to his obnoxious, autocratic boss and proclaimed, "I was too chicken to live my life, so I sold it to you for $300 a week!"

The amount of money we earn or the success we manage to achieve through our own efforts produces emptiness . . . unless it is in line with a purpose beyond ourselves.

> Miserable are the persons who do not have something beyond themselves to search for. (Charles Allen)

We can sell ourselves for such and such an amount per week . . . or spend it on a valuable investment of purpose, direction, and eternal, long-lasting goals. To experience anything approaching success in the truest meaning of the word will require this daily consistency of continuing to do what we should be doing. It is finding purpose in being reliable, in being trustworthy, being counted on time and time again by ourselves as well as others. It's looking beyond ourselves to see the ultimate, eternal goal and doing every day what is needed to achieve it.

The future is flexible, waiting to be shaped by you! Faith is believing in God, believing in the future, believing in success in such a way as to translate the mental and spoken faith into consistent actions. This kind of commitment is concerned about working with our faith as expressed in our faithfulness to make the future agree with our desires, desires that are expressed in God's Word.

Danne and Jorge Martinez wanted to raise their 11-year-old daughter, Lizbet, to do the right thing. They wanted her to have values that were sound and moral.

Unfortunately, they had no choice but to teach Lizbet to lie.

You see, the Martinez family lived in Cuba. They were members of Castro's Communist Party. They had no choice but to play by the Party's rules. Inside their home, though, Danne and Jorge complained bitterly about the political situation that was destroying their country. And so, when Lizbet was old enough to attend school, her parents sat her down and explained to her the facts of life. She was never to publicly criticize the Communist system. She was never to tell anyone what her parents talked about at home. If her teacher said anything that contradicted what her parents taught her, she was to keep her mouth shut. Danne and Jorge loathed the fact that they had to teach Lizbet to lie, but it was necessary for the survival of the family.

Fortunately, Lizbet was an extremely bright child and she learned her lesson well. Not only was Lizbet bright, she also had an astonishing talent for music. She was chosen to be the first violinist of the Havana youth symphony.

It was primarily for Lizbet's sake that Danne and Jorge decided to escape to the United States. They knew that they could never get a visa, so Jorge began swiping inner tubes from a nearby trucking depot. Finally, in August 1994 word came that security along the beaches had been cut back, and it was safer to escape now. Danne and Jorge knew that if they were ever going to go, they would have to go now. They would build a raft out of inner tubes and set out for the States. But this was dangerous, and so Jorge and Danne thought they should consult Lizbet. When Jorge and Danne told Lizbet of their plan, she left the room. She came back with her Bible, her violin, and her asthma inhaler. "I'm ready," she said.

Lizbet was ready to begin this journey to a new life. That night the Martinez family and ten other people climbed aboard the inner tube raft and set out on the Caribbean. For six days they were at sea, beaten by the burning sun and the high waves. In the early morning of the sixth day they were all picked up by a U.S. Coast Guard ship. As Lizbet climbed aboard the ship, she wanted so much to thank these officers for rescuing her family, but she was unable to speak English. So Lizbet took out her violin and began playing a song she had been secretly practicing in her room for so long . . . "The Star Spangled Banner."

For her, and her family, America's national anthem was a symbol of her new life of freedom. They believed in freedom and consistently made the preparations until one day they were able to stand in freedom on the deck of one of our ships! Success based on faith and faithfulness, faith and reliability!

> ## THE REWARD OF A TASK FAITHFULLY DONE IS BEING CALLED TO A LARGER TASK!

Chapter 5

True Success and the Getaway Principle

*Success is to be measured not so much
by the position one has reached in life
. . . but rather as the circumstances from
which he or she has escaped from on the
road to success!*

My father came to America as an immigrant at the age of 18. Growing up as a boy, I often asked, "Dad, why did you come to America?" The answers I got varied as to my age, but always the one constant was this reply, "I came to America so I could be free to start my life all over again." Success to my father was an escape from the bondage of his heritage, an escape to be able to do as he wanted with his life, to be free to make his choice as to his life vocation without having to adhere to family expectations. He wanted to be free from the limitations of his country's political system. Coming to America was almost a sacred act for him. His becoming a naturalized citizen was a privilege he never took for granted as his sons tended to do.

Success has been pictured for us as a ladder which

can be climbed to achievement. Let's broaden that view to include that success, in reality, is a way to escape, a way out, a fire escape, an evacuation route. It's much more than being a winner . . . it is the end of being a loser. Success is the way out of a difficult past, out of failure, out of poverty, out of hard times, out of bondage, out of the prisons which we have created by our faulty thinking. It's getting out from under the load — it's being set free!

A small businessman, an immigrant from the old country, kept his accounts payable in a cigar box, his accounts receivable on a spindle, and his cash in the cash register. His son, who had gone away to college, returned and said, "Dad, I don't see how you can run your business this way. How do you know what your profits are?"

This naturalized businessman replied, "Son, when I got off the boat, searching for freedom to make a profit, hoping to find a new life, I had only the pants I was wearing. Today your sister is a computer programmer and CEO, your brother is a doctor, and you're studying to be an accountant. I have two cars, a nice home, and a good business. Everything is paid for. So you add it all up, subtract the pants, and there's your profit!"

> To ESCAPE is simply another way of expressing SUCCESS!

This is one of the major themes of the Bible . . . God making a way to escape, God providing a way to escape! You see it from the very beginning in principle. The earth "escaped" the chaos and became ordered. Out of darkness came the light! This is the bottom-line principle of what salvation is all about. This is why Jesus Christ was sent to live among people so He could die for people, taking their condemnation of sin and death, allowing each of us to escape the penalty of death to eternal life! It's seen everywhere! This is what God is all about!

> We have *escaped* like a bird out of the fowler's snare; the snare has been broken, and we have *escaped*. Our help is in the name of the Lord, the Maker of heaven and earth (Ps. 124:7-8, emphasis added).

You've heard it said, "The Greeks have a word for it." Well, in this case, the Spanish have a word for it. Not always is the English language as expressive or the best suited to give us clarity about success. The Spanish word for success is our word for "fire escape" . . . EXITO! In Spanish, "success" equals "exito" and in our terms it is the EXIT sign! Every time you see this sign posted in a public building . . . be reminded of this meaning of success. Success is finding and knowing where the exit is. In the case of a fire . . . it means exit is the way to life, to reach a breath of fresh air, to get out of the way of danger. Then when we understand that "success" is a way out, it becomes something attainable for each of us! Success is not only to be experienced by gifted or special people . . . it's something on the bottom shelf, something for all of us.

What is it that success can help you escape from? God's true kinds of success have to do with escaping . . . a breaking from the past which has held us as a prisoner. The prison holding you can be poverty, fear, lack of knowledge, lousy attitude, faulty thinking, abusive situations, fear of failure, not understanding what true biblical success is, or . . . ? Whatever is holding you from being a success is something from which you can escape with God's help and God's plan! This is one reason why success is so much more than how much money you may have or what position you may have attained.

Maybe this is the point at which to deal with not

only the fear of failure but the fear of success. Yes, too many of God's good people are concerned about experiencing success. They are fearful that if they have too much success or too much money that these things will change them for the worse. It's a legitimate fear to overcome, for some people. This fear of success allows people to trust God to be poor and defeated but not to trust God for anything more out of life. They want everyone to share the poverty but not the abundance of God.

A long time ago, at a time in history when poverty was the expected lifestyle for the majority of people, Paul the Apostle penned one of the healthiest, best-balanced concepts for a successful life that I have ever read:

> Make it your ambition to lead a quiet life, to mind your own business and to work with your hands, just as we told you, so that your daily life may win the respect of outsiders and so that *you will not be dependent on anybody* (1 Thess. 4:11-12, emphasis added).

There you have it . . . succinct, to the point, a success plan for God's people: A self-sufficiency with the blessing of God and the respect of others! What will success be for you? Again, God has success in mind for all of us! When you make your escape to this kind of balanced living, you are not the only to be blessed. Your neighbors, family, associates, and friends all are benefited, too, because of the respect earned.

The Bible is absolutely chock-full of "escape" stories — many more than we have the space in which to share them all with you. But how about taking note of a few. As you work your way down through them, please note at least two things: The person or persons doing the escaping benefited themselves and, in their escape, others also received benefit.

• ABRAHAM escaped the comforts of the land of Ur in order to live in tents so that he could be the recipient of God's plan and consequently the blessings of God for him as well as for all of his offspring. Because of this escape, God made of him a great nation . . . blessing all the peoples of the earth, all the way down to us, today.

• LOT barely managed to escape from the judgment poured out on Sodom and Gomorrah because of the kindness of God to whom Abraham had interceded for Lot's life and the life of his family.

• NOAH escaped the ravages of the flood when he listened to God's plan for his escape. He and his family survived to re-establish the animal family as well as the human family upon this earth.

• JOSEPH escaped from the pit into which he had been thrown by his brothers so that he lived to later allow their escape from the famine which could have destroyed them at a later date.

• MOSES escaped the edict of death for all boy babies so that later he could become the deliverer of his people so they could escape from Egyptian bondage.

• DAVID defeated the giant Goliath to allow the nation of Israel to be freed from the Philistine bondage.

• Dis-enfranchised people who were burdened by the past escaped to join the cause of David in the caves. These men later formed the core of an army that would follow him all the way to the king-ship of Israel. This escape to living in a cave marked the end of their losing ways.

**JESUS escaped the fury and death threats of Herod as his mother and father fled to Egypt as directed by an angel.

**PETER escaped the prison of King Herod so that he could continue with the successful ministry given to him.

**PAUL the Apostle escaped arrest in Damascus when he was lowered in a basket through a window so he could continue his ministry to others.

**ALL OF US . . . YOU AND ME . . . have the privilege of escaping the corruption in this world through the knowledge, biblical promises, and the ultimate sacrifice of Jesus Christ on a cross to receive a rich welcome into the eternal kingdom of God!

The Bible is the ultimate, final word on "escaping"! God allows escaping and makes a way in which it can happen, so that His people can escape the hard times, judgments, and plots against them so they can survive. Why survive? So they can help others to also escape. How else can we survive bad times? In the escapes, we have just been reminded that God allowed His followers to escape armies, angry people, famines, tough times, reversals, sin, death, arrests, bondage, angry people, threatening situations, and all kinds of things. God makes a way to escape!

Perhaps the ultimate question of escape was framed like this:

> For if the message spoken by angels was binding, and every violation and disobedience received its just punishment, *how shall we escape if we ignore such a*

great salvation? This salvation, which was
first announced by the Lord, was confirmed
to us by those who heard him. God also
testified to it by signs, wonders and vari-
ous miracles, and gifts of the Holy Spirit
(Heb. 2:2-4, emphasis added).

Success really starts with an escape! And that success begins with a decision, a choice!

Do you want to "escape" to something better than
your present situation?

An example of problems which can result from decisions is illustrated by the two vets from the Vietnam War
who pooled their money and started a small business
canning salmon in the Pacific Northwest. It didn't take
long for the partners to realize they had a problem with
their processing . . . every time a customer opened a
can, the fish inside was gray in color.

The partner who handled the marketing put a lot of
pressure on his friend, "Come on, you're the technical
guy. Fix it!"

The technical partner studied the problem and later
replied, "I can fix it but it will take lots of money and
some time."

The marketing guy replied, "Look, if we can't fix it
quickly, let's feature it!" That day they changed the label
to read: "THE ONLY SALMON GUARANTEED NOT TO
TURN PINK IN THE CAN!"

So . . . WHY DOES GOD ALLOW SUCCESS?

God has lots of reasons for providing avenues of escape so that some of His people can experience success.
For instance, how can people survive crop failures, mar-
ket collapses, wars, plagues, disease, disaster . . . unless
some of His people have been successful enough in the
present to set something aside with which to survive the
hard times! Success allows a surplus to be set aside. If no

one were successful . . . no one would survive hard times!

Let's look at another biblical example: Why did Joseph end up in Egypt? Why did he escape the plans to kill him by his brothers? If you remember that part of history . . . ultimately, Joseph, through lots of testing and circumstances and the blessing of God on his life, interpreted the dream of the pharaoh. The dream simply visualized for the king the coming of hard times. In order to survive, the plan would be to have seven excellent, successful years with a proportion of that surplus being set aside for the seven lean years which were coming. Joseph survived and became a success in order to become the man God would use to bless and protect and preserve His people Israel. Without Joseph and those good years of surplus, how would there have been an escape of disaster? The whole world became dependent upon the success of seven good years and the wisdom of a man like Joseph who, under God's blessing, knew how to handle and provide for the hard times coming.

When he was age 19, Dean Kamen designed a cigar box-sized pump to help his brother, a medical student, conduct experiments on laboratory animals. He built it in the basement workshop of his family's Long Island home. The pump worked so well that Kamen's brother showed it to the professor, who used it in his own experiments. When the professor wrote up the experiment in a medical journal, giving credit to the younger Kamen, Dean's phone began ringing with calls from scientists around the world.

Soon Dean Kamen dropped out of college to keep up with the demand. Gradually, as he perfected his pumps and learned how to down-size them, he perceived another customer group that also needed a small, reliable, light-weight pump. Diabetics could use such a pump to monitor the presence of glucose in the bloodstream and inject insulin to counteract it.

The success of Dean allows others to escape the ravages of diabetes. The successful actions of one person can allow lots of others to also experience success. Now that's what success is all about, in God's plans for humanity.

Stop a moment and think about how America came into being. America was originally settled by people who were making an escape! What were they escaping from? They came to escape religious persecutions, anti-Semitism, poverty, famines, bondage from oppressive political systems, forced militarism, forced occupations, forced marriages, and more. Their escaping built for all of us a wonderful land of opportunity. Americans are nothing more than a whole bunch of escapees. Our nation, this land of the free, this land where all are free to pursue life, liberty, and happiness, is encouragement for all of us to continue to pursue this success. Success for the few is an absolute necessity so that all of us can survive. It's the way to provide something better. It's a coming out from under.

One of the most powerful scenes from the movie "Lawrence of Arabia" depicts the ten-day death march that Lawrence's army made through the desert. As the army staggered along, nearly dead from dehydration, they suddenly spied an oasis and eagerly fell into the water, drinking it. When Lawrence took a head count, he noticed that one of the camel boys was missing. The boy's camel was found riderless near the back of the camp. Lawrence immediately told his men, "We must go back and find him."

But the men refused to venture back into the merciless furnace of sand. "Master," they pleaded, "it is Allah's will that the boy did not return with us. His fate was written by God. We must not interfere."

Lawrence angrily re-mounted his camel and headed back into the sand dunes. The men stood there shaking their heads. "Now, we've lost him, too," they said as they returned to their rest and new-found water.

Two days later, a shimmering image emerged from the heat waves. "It's Lawrence! He's found the boy!" the soldiers shouted as they ran to assist him.

Lawrence leaned over and handed them the unconscious boy. He looked into their faces and said in a hoarse whisper: "Remember this: NOTHING IS WRITTEN UNLESS YOU WRITE IT!"

Success is more than a ladder to the top! Success is a way out, an escape to something better! Success which is personal also allows others to be blessed so that they, too, can experience an escape! Success is coming out from under the problems of the past to move into a bright new future! The Bible encourages us to escape from our past so that we can experience a wonderful eternal reward!

Her name is Thelma Boston, and as far as Zig Ziglar (motivational speaker) is concerned, she is the "Mother Teresa" of South Dallas, Texas. In September of 1969, Thelma's husband was murdered and the future looked pretty bleak. However, Thelma is a remarkable person when it comes to such things as love and faith.

To this date, Thelma has had a hand in the rearing of more than 200 foster kids. She has kept up to 14 at a time. The children Thelma gets are those nobody else wants. Some are severely mentally disadvantaged, others have physical problems that could break your heart. However, when Thelma gets these kids, miracles take place! Success happens! Escape becomes possible! Many of them come from a background of extreme abuse — physical, sexual, psychological, and mental. They're male and female, black, white, Hispanic, and just about everything else in between.

Twenty-two-year-old Jonathan, who has the mental alertness of a nine year old is but one example. Jonathan had established quite a reputation in 20 different foster homes and nobody wanted him! But that's the kind of a kid Thelma seeks out. Lots of kids who function at much lower levels than Jonathan are accepted at other homes. Jonathan was unwanted because he did things that are socially unacceptable. "Little" things like waking up in the middle of the night, walking over to his room-mate's bed and spitting or urinating in his face. "Little" things like choking the neighbor's cat to death. In short, Jonathan was not the kind of child who was welcomed. Now he is one more of Thelma's "miracle" kids, acting like a gentleman, no more socially unacceptable behaviors, the picture of politeness and good behavior.

Then, there's Marco Evans who is a teenager about three feet tall. He's in bed most of the time because his physical condition doesn't give him any options. His bones are extremely soft and therefore he cannot stand up. Marco is a bright, articulate kid who reaches up and grabs the heart of just about everyone who sees him. The influence he has and the respect he enjoys from the other kids is remarkable. As you watch Thelma talk to him and you see his bright-eyed optimism, you can't help but be encouraged and excited.

If you were to ask Thelma her secret of success, she would answer with modesty, grace, and faith. Hear her as she says, "I just love 'em and I trust the Lord."

She is making an escape possible for these kids!

> While David was playing the harp, Saul tried to pin him to the wall with his spear, but David eluded him as Saul drove the spear into the wall. *That night David made good his escape* (1 Sam. 19:9-10, emphasis added).

> And David knew that the Lord had established him as king over Israel and had

exalted his kingdom *for the sake of his people Israel* (2 Sam. 5:12, emphasis added).

SUCCESS IS JUDGED NOT BY WHAT WE HAVE . . . BUT BY HOW MANY WE HAVE HELPED!

Chapter 6

True Success and the Integrity Principle

Integrity cannot be purchased, bargained for, inherited, rented, or imported from afar . . . it must be home grown!

Danny Sutton, eight years old, wrote the following for his third grade Sunday school teacher, who had asked her students to explain God:

One of God's main jobs is making people. He makes these to put in the place of the ones who die so there will be enough people to take care of things here on earth. He doesn't make grownups, He just makes babies. I think because they are smaller and easier to make. That way He doesn't have to take up His valuable time teaching them to walk and talk. He can just leave that up to the mothers and fathers. I think it works out pretty good.

God's second most important job is listening to prayers. An awful lot of this goes on, 'cause some people, like preachers and things, pray other times besides bedtimes, and Grandpa and Grandma pray every time they eat, except for snacks.

God sees and hears everything and is everywhere, which keeps Him pretty busy. So you shouldn't go wasting His time asking for things that aren't important, or go over parents' heads and ask for something they said you couldn't have. It doesn't work anyway.

Sounds to me as though eight-year-old Danny has about got it right — "God's main job is making people!" But considering the subject at hand, we — YOU and ME — need to be part of the process as well. There is no true success to enjoy without INTEGRITY! The kinds of success that God is interested in is always attained with and through integrity of person and integrity of character. No short cuts are allowed on this road to success. No corner-cutting is allowed, no dishonesty, no excuses, and no easy ways out.

What does the word "integrity" mean? The word itself comes from the word "integer" which means a whole number as contrasted with a fraction. It means wholeness; soundness; unimpairedness; consistent, firm adherence to a code of values; no division; uprightness; honesty; and moral perfection.

Such qualities seem to be in very short supply today. We are never quite sure what we can believe from people in politics. There is no assurance that the private, hidden, character of the person matches up with the public image portrayed. People are questioning a whole lot of things. Even the church has come under scrutiny today. The business world is under siege. Can we really trust big companies or for that matter, little companies? Who can you trust today? The essential ingredients of integrity are truth and honesty. This word "integrity" describes a person whose character and lifestyle and words are all of the same quality.

At bedtime, Lillian Holcomb told her two grandsons a Bible story, then asked if they knew what the word "sin" meant. Seven-year-old Keith spoke up: "It's when you do something real bad."

Four-year-old Aaron's eyes widened and he said, "I know a big sin Keith did today."

Annoyed, Keith turned to his little brother: "You take care of your sins and I'll take care of mine."

Oh, yes, it is your responsibility to take care of your own integrity!

#1: INTEGRITY IS TO BE ON THE INSIDE AS WELL AS ON THE OUTSIDE!

Life is to be consistent . . . consistently good, inside and out. Integrity conveys the meaning of something that is integrated. All of the same quality. People in general know that they ought to be consistent in character, even if they do not achieve it. They judge other people by this standard of consistency. This is one of the values highly prized by the Bible.

When a new king was about to be chosen by the prophet Samuel, he had been guided and directed to go to the household of Jesse and there he was introduced to all of Jesse's fine, good-looking, strapping sons, except one. We can pick up the story when they arrived. Samuel saw Eliab and thought, *Surely the Lord's anointed stands here before the Lord.* And here is the crux of the matter:

> But the Lord said to Samuel, "Do not consider his appearance or his height, for I have rejected him. The Lord does not look

at the things man looks at. *Man looks at the outward appearance, but the Lord looks at the heart.*" (1 Sam. 16:6-7, emphasis added).

So the choice was made . . . not any of the six sons paraded before Samuel . . . but the chosen one was still out tending the sheep, little brother, overlooked by dad and the older brothers.

Jesus made the very same distinction. He pointedly was critical of the Pharisees because of their outward show of religiosity when their inward attitudes were lousy. They were teaching and putting great stress on being pure by ritually washing their hands and bodies when inwardly they had violent and selfish attitudes. Jesus reminded them that if they had purified their attitudes and inner self there would be no more need for the ceremonial washing of hands. A clean, pure heart would lead to clean actions. This thing of integrity means being pure on the inside as well as on the outside.

Billy Graham, speaking to a world conference of national evangelists, declared that our world today is looking for men and women of integrity. Several months later in an interview, the word popped up again: "Graham says he will be content with a simple epitaph for his life and ministry: 'A sinner saved by grace; a man who, like the Psalmist, walked in his integrity. I'd like people to remember that I had integrity.' "[3]

It's what's on the inside, the moral compass, the center from which all actions spring, that is important. If honesty and truth are not to be found there . . . how can it be expressed outwardly in inter-personal relationships?

Woe to you, teachers of the law and Pharisees, you hypocrites! You clean the outside of the cup and dish, but inside they are full of greed and self-indulgence. Blind

> Pharisee! First clean the inside of the cup
> and dish, and then the outside also will be
> clean (Matt. 23:25-26).

A four-year-old-girl was at the pediatrician's office for a checkup. As the doctor looked into her ears with an otoscope, he asked, "Do you think I'll find Big Bird in here?" She remained silent. Next, the doctor took a tongue depressor and looked down her throat and asked, "Do you think I'll find the Cookie Monster down here?" Again, she was silent. Then the doctor put a stethoscope to her chest. As he listened to her heartbeat, he asked, "Do you think I'll hear Barney in here?"

"Oh, no!" she replied, "Jesus is in my heart. Barney's on my underpants!"

2: INTEGRITY HAS TO DO WITH MOTIVES AND ACTIONS

In no way am I implying that outward actions don't count. To be a person of integrity means that our hearts are pure AND that our outward lives are lived in the same way. Are the outward actions congruent with our inward motives? The outward actions always express what is on the inside.

Back to the example of the hypocritical Pharisees. They were in the habit of saying long prayers in public, gaining a reputation for being religious. These hypocrites then used their reputations to entice widows to trust to them the legal care of their estates, which they abused by misappropriating the funds. Here's the indictment: As He taught, Jesus said, "Watch out for the teachers of the law. They like to walk around in flowing robes and be greeted in the marketplaces, and have the most important seats in the synagogues and the place of honor at banquets. They devour widows' houses and for a show make lengthy prayers. Such men will be punished most severely" (Mark 12:38-40).

There are lots of words that describe integrity, all of which are synonymous in part. Yet this character trait can absorb them all and still have room for more. But the words describing the opposite of integrity often begin with a "d": devious, deceitful, dissembling, double-talk, double-minded, duplicitous, and the devil. Whatever its definition, we are more concerned about what integrity looks like when draped with sinew, muscle, and skin. What comes out of it? What ideas will it give birth to? What actions will integrity trigger? That's our more important concern. With integrity on the inside what will these people look like on the outside with their actions for all to see?

This world in which we live places a premium on the outward appearance . . . clothes make the person . . . sporting the latest looks in fashion . . . modeling the latest hairdo . . . driving the right kind of transportation . . . living in the correct neighborhood . . . being seen with the right people. It's a shallow way of judging when the Bible says, "Your beauty should not come from outward adornment, such as . . . wearing of gold jewelry and fine clothes. Instead, it should be that of your inner self, the unfading beauty of a gentle and quiet spirit, which is of great worth in God's sight" (1 Pet. 3:3-4).

We cannot make the mistake of assuming that only the inward matters and the outward doesn't matter. To be a person of integrity means that the two sides, motives and actions, will always be in harmony with each other. What is your inner guide? How does this translate in living?

Dave Brown, a Seattle Seahawk (National Football League) and a Christian, plays the safety position. A few years ago he fell on tough times in the early part of one season. He was burned, as they say, a number of times. He gave up big plays for big scores. The press and public were definitely on his case. When interviewed about his play, he said, "I don't have any animosity toward the fans or the writers for what was written. There is no one in the game who can't get beat. I know what I can do. I know what I am. I am a man of God."

One of his teammates said, "He's a winner. He has such confidence in himself."

Another teammate added, "He could have laid down, but he didn't. His personal beliefs are so strong."

Brown's inner strength and integrity guided and preserved him. He knew what he was on the inside and in his actions and responses he was true to himself. To the person of integrity, motives and actions are in harmony!

#3: INTEGRITY IS WORDS AND DEEDS THAT FOLLOW!

Having just looked at the fact that integrity must be in our motives and actions . . . let's take that one step further. In particular, our WORDS and DEEDS must be consistent with each other.

> Dear children, let us not love with
> words or tongue but with ACTIONS and in
> TRUTH (1 John 3:18, emphasis added).

Words can be wonderful and comforting and helpful . . . but words alone are not enough when the situation can only be remedied with deeds expressed in a tangible way.

The word "integrity" is used 19 times in the New International Version (NIV) of the Old Testament. Most of these uses are in biographical sketches that make integrity come alive before us in flesh and blood. David learned the meaning of this word. After he had completed the fund raising for the temple which Solomon would later build, he prayed, "But who am I, and who are my people, that we should be able to give as generously as this? Everything comes from you, and we have given you only what comes from your hand" (1 Chron. 29:14). This is the man, David, that God had forged and shaped. But his next words reveal his heart even more: "I know, my God, that you test the heart and are pleased with integrity. All these things have I given willingly and with honest intent" (1 Chron. 29:17). Not only did he say it, but the deeds which followed and accompanied his words were one and the same.

Speaking of David, we can follow his concern about integrity being the mark of his lifestyle. He was willing to allow God to evaluate him on the basis of his integrity: "Judge me, O Lord, according to my righteousness, according to my integrity" (Ps. 7:8). He even prayed: "May integrity and uprightness protect me" (Ps. 25:21).

Job was often cited for his patience and endurance, but I nominate him for one of the most exciting examples of integrity found anywhere. Here is one of the most powerful recommendations ever given to anybody — God is the first to reference Job's integrity: "Have you considered my servant Job? There is no one on earth like him; he is blameless and upright, a man who fears God and shuns evil. And he still maintains his INTEGRITY, though you incited me against him to ruin him without any reason" (Job 2:3, emphasis added). When his suffering was at its worst, his wife taunted him, "Are you still holding on to your INTEGRITY? Curse God and die!" (Job 2:9, emphasis added).

As the problems piled up and woes seemed to multiply and even his friends turned against him, Job still held to his conviction: "I will never admit you are in the right; till I die, I will not deny my INTEGRITY" (Job 27:5, emphasis added). Job held on to his integrity so that his thoughts and words were of the same quality through testing, trials, temptations, taunts, and finally through triumph!

The Book of Job is really a manual on true success. The book begins with his being one of the richest men on the face of the earth . . . then disaster strikes . . . to be followed by a time of testing, wondering, waiting . . . to be concluded by restoration. Job ended up with twice as much in the way of success as was his at the beginning. Why? One major element in his life was his integrity . . . in good times and in bad times, in thick and in thin, in good and in disaster . . . Job held on to his integrity!

Here's the ultimate test of integrity: "In all this, Job did not sin by charging God with wrongdoing" (Job 1:22). And here it is again, repeated, "In all this, Job did not sin in WHAT HE SAID" (Job 2:10, emphasis added). Words and deeds cannot be separated! By the words we say, we reveal what is on the inside.

> What you become is far more important than what you get. What you get will be influenced by what you become! (Jim Rohn)

In many ways, integrity is the life quality that places its stamp of approval on all the other good qualities of life. To fail at integrity is to fail at everything else. You can be talented, knowledgeable, capable, gifted, successful, and have remarkable abilities. However, if you are not believed to be a person of integrity, you will not be trusted. You will eventually fail. Cleverness and brilliance can take you a long way in public life, for a time, but in the long run it all fails miserably unless the brilliance is matched by the character trait of integrity.

> ## #4: INTEGRITY HAS TO DO
> ## WITH GOD AND OTHER PEOPLE!

If our inside and outside, if our motives and actions, if our words and deeds must all be integrated . . . then, too, so must our attitudes toward God and toward other people! One of the real glaring fissures in character is found here — people who profess to love God can fail in living out that same kind of love to other people. Here is the major point of experiencing true success. It must not be achieved at the expense of others. It must not be sought after by stepping on others. This relationship is explicit in the Word of God. Read it again:

> If anyone says, "I love God," yet hates his brother, he is a liar. For anyone who does not love his brother, whom he has seen, cannot love God, whom he has not seen. And He has given us this command: WHO-EVER LOVES GOD MUST ALSO LOVE HIS BROTHER (1 John 4:20-21, emphasis added).

John, the writer, was all too conscious of this happening in his church where there was much emphasis on loving God . . . and even talk of loving other people . . . and yet, apparently, these people did not love each other. This kind of behavior is inconsistent and shows a lack of real integrity.

Jesus, the ultimate example of a person of integrity, linked together these two great commandments: To love God and to love our neighbors! To illustrate this, He told the most famous parable of all, about a most unlikely person to model this behavior. Today we call him "The Good Samaritan." But in his day, the Samaritans were utterly despised by the Jews, considered nothing but dogs, people who were to be spit on. This Samaritan is the prime example of God's plan for successful living. Jesus took this apparently successful businessman, from the most unpopular social minority and told his audience, as well as us to "GO AND DO LIKEWISE!"

Perhaps we should explore this a bit more. Consider that this good Samaritan was not part of the idle rich of his day. He worked hard for his living, he spent nights on the road away from his family. No one else helped him travel between Jericho and Jerusalem. He owned a means of transportation, he had some money in his purse, he had good credit. Could he be the example of success which sounds more like the American way than any other biblical character?

Notice . . . this Samaritan example of success had the obstacles of wrong race, wrong education, wrong religion. He simply had the right methods, right goals, right kind of integrity, and right attitude for becoming a success in his business life and personal life. He was a man of integrity . . . what he was on the inside was lived out on the outside. His motives and his actions were integrated. He is the example of using his success as God has intended it to be used. He shared the success that was his, he was willing to help someone in need who had been ignored by others, particularly the religious types so often referred to by Jesus. For being this kind of a man of integrity . . . Jesus commended him . . . and told us to go and do the same thing!

If you are a bit fuzzy about the details, perhaps this would be a good time to give it another read . . . find this exciting story of integrity, love for God and love for a neighbor in Luke's account, chapter ten.

It is being a hypocrite to listen to God's commandments to love Him but to fail to apply the same kind of love to our neighbors. Success is not a solo flight! Success has a vertical as well as a horizontal dimension to it.

> The Christian should be a man with an absolute integrity towards truth in every discipline. He will ignore no serious questions, he will keep abreast of contemporary issues and face problems squarely, tackling some immediately and placing others in cold storage until he has the time and strength to wrestle them through. (Os Guinness)

Nearly every critical issue in our society today is connected to a problem involving integrity or the lack of it. In our time we have seen statesmanship become politics, music become noise, enthusiasm become cynicism, love become sex, immorality become preference, and sin become choice. It has become so bad that today, some of the cynical, liberal leaders are now calling for a return to integrity and subsequently, moral principles by which this society can survive! Never has there been a day or time when integrity is more desperately needed. We need to live out in real life these qualities. When integrated into our living it will affect individual lifestyles as well as corporate lifestyles.

Let's just consider in one specific area where a life of integrity would immediately effect lifestyle changes. Dr. Paul Cameron and colleagues conducted research on 6,714 obituaries from 16 USA homosexual/gay journals from 1981 through 1995 and compared the same size sample to obituaries from regular newspapers. The sampling from newspapers matched the USA averages for longevity. The median age of death of married men was age 75; 80 percent of whom died at age 65 or older. The median age of death of unmarried or divorced men was 57; 32 percent of whom died at age 65 or older. The median age of death for married women was 79; 85 percent of whom died at 65 or older. The median age of death of unmarried or divorced women was 71; 60 percent of whom died at 65 or older.

But the comparison of these statistics to the homosexual population is startling. Less than 2 percent of the homosexuals surveyed survived to age 65! For homosexuals with AIDS the median age at death was 39. For those whose death was from other factors, other than AIDS, the median age at death was 42. The survey also found that of the lesbians studied, their median age of death was 45. Only 23 percent of those survived to the age of 65 or older. Other factors about the homosexual community were also alarming. Homosexuals are 116 times more likely to be murdered and 24 times more likely to commit suicide when compared to the non-homosexual community.

Webster's dictionary gives three choices when defining integrity: 1) An unimpaired condition; 2) firm adherence to a code of especially moral or artistic values; and 3) the quality or state of being complete or undivided. So among other things, integrity is a firm adherence to a code of moral values. That ultimate code is Bible based . . . beginning with the TEN COMMANDMENTS.

Pressures to let go of one's integrity will come from family, friends, peers, fellow workers, society, or the media. There will be many pressures — political, economic, emotional, religious, and physical —to compromise, give up, or let go of our integrity when faced with tough times. You can hold fast to what is right!

Now . . . it's time for some of those "white-knuckle" kinds of questions:

- Are you a person who keeps your word?
- Will you refuse to compromise on your integrity when under stress?

- Do you fulfill your commitments and are you de-
  voted to your duties?
- Are you in a constant, untiring pursuit of the truth?
- Do you speak the truth no matter what people want
  to hear?
- Is your life marked by undivided love and obedi-
  ence to God?
- Could others describe you as a person of unim-
  paired condition morally?
- Will you adhere to an inner code of ethics that is
  complete and undivided?
- Are you who you say you are?
- What characteristics do you have that you think
  mark you as a person of integrity?
- What characteristics do you have that you think
  detract from your integrity?

You might be thinking about now, *This is a huge load
to dump on me at one time.* Which can be followed by
another question that is also bothering you: "HOW CAN
I EVER BECOME A PERSON OF INTEGRITY?"

On the human level, this is probably an impossible
assignment. We need help in becoming a person of integrity. The source of all true integrity is in God himself.
However, as your life is committed to honesty in relationship with God and your fellow persons, be assured
that your choice will be reinforced by God. He sent His
only Son to pay a price so that we can become people of
integrity. There is help! By His power we can become
the people of integrity!

Fast-forward with me to the end of your life. Think . . .
when you die and the people are filing out of the church
or funeral home after your memorial service, what will
they be commenting on about your life? Will they say,
"You sure knew where she stood," or "He said what he
meant and meant what he said," or "You could count on

her?" or "You could trust him!" Will anybody say, "THAT WAS A PERSON OF INTEGRITY!"?

The very wealthy English Baron Fitzgerald had only one son, who was the apple of his eye, the center of attention and love. The son grew up, his wife died, then this son, also became sick and died. Fitzgerald grieved over this double loss. But in the meantime his holdings and investments and wealth increased, life moved on. He used much of his wealth to acquire a wonderful collection of the artworks of the "masters."

He had prepared his will ahead of his own death. When that time came, to settle the estate, all of his art collection was to be sold, as he had directed in his will. Because of the quality and the quantity of the art in this collection, which was valued in the millions of pounds, a huge crowd of buyers gathered, expectantly.

There was however, one painting which received little attention because it was of poor quality and painted by some unknown artist. It happened to be a portrait of Fitzgerald's son.

When the auctioneer was ready . . . the bidding was to begin. The attorney read first from the will of Fitzgerald which instructed that the first painting to be sold was the painting of "my beloved son."

The poor quality painting didn't receive any bidders . . . except one! The only bidder was the old servant who had known the son and loved him and served him. For less than an English pound he bid and, being the only bidder, out of sentimental reasons he bought the painting.

The auction was stopped for the attorney to continue reading from the will of Fitzgerald these words: "Whoever buys my son gets it all. The auction is over!"

And, whoever gets Jesus Christ, the only Son of God, the supreme model of integrity gets it all . . . including INTEGRITY!

Frank Gaebelein, founder of the Stony Brook School in New York and a co-founder of *Christianity Today*, was a man of integrity. His daughter Gretchen Gaebelein Hull writes:

> Long before I knew how to spell the word or even knew what it meant, I realized my father was a man of integrity. Later, I would learn phrases like "Christian commitment" and "devotion to duty," but from my earliest years I simply knew that Frank Gaebelein "rang true."
>
> My sister and brother and I saw that as our dad sought to obey the commands of the Lord, his private life was consistent with his public images, a man of moral and intellectual integrity. Dad knew that a person of integrity can be well-meaning but rigid . . . even legalistic . . . if he does not understand that maintaining integrity includes the difficult and continuing effort of discerning truth.[4]

Chapter 7

True Success and the Priority Principle

Life is like a coin . . . you can spend it any
way you wish, but you can spend it only
once! (Charles R. Swindoll)

One of the most fascinating stories in sports is the story of an eight-year-old boy who told everybody who would listen, "I am going to be the greatest baseball catcher that ever lived."

People laughed at him and said, "Dream on, you silly boy." His mother cautioned him, "You are only eight years old, that's not the time to be talking of an impossible dream." At his high school graduation, he walked across the stage to receive his diploma and the superintendent of schools stopped him and said, "Johnny, tell these people what you want to be."

The young man squared his shoulders and said, "I am going to be the greatest baseball catcher that ever lived." And you could hear snickers across that crowd.

The late Casey Stengel, when asked about this baseball catcher, said, "Johnny Bench is probably already the greatest baseball catcher that ever played this game."

During his career, among other awards, twice he was voted the "outstanding" player of the year. A priority was set which allowed this kind of accomplishment and record to be established.

Choosing one thing above all the many choices we are faced with in life is not easy for most of us. The possibilities are endless! The choices are myriad! A priority is simply determining what comes FIRST!

If you ever hope to make a real success out of your life, you will be forced to make difficult choices. Think of the possibilities . . . some are good, some are bad . . . and a very few will be the best.

> WHAT WILL BE FIRST IN MY LIFE?
> WHAT IS MY REAL REASON FOR LIVING?
> WHAT PRIORITY WILL HAVE
> FIRST PLACE IN MY LIFE?

We don't have to look very far for the answers! In making these choices it really comes down to only two . . . will we or will we not? The TOP PRIORITIES for living have already been chosen, selected by the ultimate source of truth in the universe. Jesus Christ himself has already stated for us what should be the top priority in life:

> But seek FIRST His kingdom and His
> righteousness, and all these things will be
> given to you as well (Matt. 6:33).

There it is — simple to understand, but perhaps not so easy to put into place. He even used the same words we are using, "But seek first. . . ." That's priority! It means that first and foremost and above anything else, this is to be your FIRST pursuit! It is #1! HIS kingdom and HIS righteousness are to be first in the lifestyles of all of us.

The original Greek word for "seek" is interesting, too.

It means "to search, to strive for, to desire strongly." But this action verb also means to "keep on striving for, keep on searching after, keep on desiring." It is a continuous life action, you don't do it once and it's all over with, you do it on an ongoing basis . . . we go for this first!

The simplicity is overwhelming. You don't even have to pray about what should be first. There it is . . . now, "JUST DO IT" as the Nike ad proclaims! Once this has been established . . . then everything else that is done in life will relate to this priority. Everything else flows out of this priority. When I work, how I work, where I work . . . every other decision and choice will be looked at through the test of Matthew 6:33. How I make my money, what I do with my money, how I experience any success, what I do with my success . . . all must pass the Matthew 6:33 test. So everything else will be measured against two questions:

> IS THIS LIFE ACTION FOR HIS KINGDOM?
> HOW DOES THIS RELATE
> TO HIS RIGHTEOUSNESS?

If you want to live with right priorities . . . here is the irreplaceable, foundational truth. However, if you are not concerned about experiencing true success without guilt, you can rationalize this away, somehow. Here is the truth for all time for all people for all circumstances of living . . . "But seek FIRST!" There can be only one number one. If there are others . . . then it's no longer the first. When something is first, everything else has to be further down the list. A priority is exclusive, in your living there can be only one first place priority. And, my friend, it's already been settled. Therefore it's our responsibility to live by this and conform our pursuits in life to this priority.

If your priorities, motives, and actions are right, you

will discover this is the most exciting way to live life. It's not all drudgery. There is a new-found life principle. No matter what else you do in life, if this has been settled, you have a whole new exciting vista. Success will be yours beyond your fondest dreams! Maybe, then, your life will turn out like the following.

> I asked God for strength that I might achieve.
> I was made weak that I might learn humbly
> to obey.

> I asked God for health that I might do
> greater things.
> I was given infirmity that I might do better things.

> I asked for riches that I might be happy.
> I was given poverty that I might be wise.

> I asked for power that I might have the praise
> of men.
> I was given weakness that I might feel the
> need for God.

> I asked for all things that I might enjoy life.
> I was given life that I might enjoy all things.

> I got nothing that I asked for . . .
> but everything I had hoped for . . .

> Almost despite myself, my unspoken prayer
> was answered.
> I am among all men most richly blessed.
> (Author is unknown, but is attributed to a
> Confederate soldier)[5]

When looking back over the context of this verse (Matt. 6:33) there are other truths that we should be exploring: Who is He talking to? Who is He talking about? Who is doing and who is not seeking these things?

"For the pagans run after all these things, and your

Heavenly Father knows that you need them" (Matt. 6:32). Here he speaks of the "pagans," in other translations he talks about the "Gentiles." In other words, people who are Jewish or people who are not interested in God and His kingdom at all.

And that brings us to another question: What are "all these things" that people are running after? We can back up all the way to verse 19 to discover that Jesus is talking about "treasures" on earth and "treasures" in heaven. Or looking at it from another angle . . . it's about how to transfer these treasures on earth into the eternal store-house of heaven. Everything in this passage seems to hinge on another life principle:

> NO ONE can serve two masters. Either he will hate the one and love the other, or he will be devoted to the one and despise the other. YOU CANNOT SERVE BOTH GOD AND MONEY (Matt. 6:24, emphasis added).

Now be really careful here! JESUS DID NOT SAY IT IS IMPOSSIBLE TO BE SUCCESSFUL AND MAKE MONEY! The key to unlocking this truth is found in the word "serve"! You cannot put both God AND money into first place! It is impossible! So, my friend, the question is: who will you be "devoted" to? You can hold to one or to the other . . . but not to both, thus there is the choice that only you can make. What will be your priority? God or money? Jesus is not beating around the bush.. . . . He has a way of getting to the crux of all matters, boiling life down to simple choices.

Charles Swindoll writes: I'll never forget a conversation I had with the late Corrie ten Boom. She said, in her broken English, "I've learned that I must hold everything loosely, because when I grip it tightly, it hurts when the Father pries my fingers loose and takes it from me!"[6]

You might be thinking, *This is pretty harsh language*. Yes, the choices are stark, plain to see, easy to comprehend. But is that all there is to this? No! This letting it all go, holding loosely to things in this life can be scary.

Let's look again at where we started and read it again . . . and don't miss the last phrase. All together: "But seek first His kingdom and His righteousness, and ALL THESE THINGS WILL BE GIVEN TO YOU AS WELL!" What are "all these things"? Why do the "pagans run after all these things"? We also have the answers. According to Jesus, we are not to worry about our life; not to worry about what we will eat and drink; not to worry about what we will wear. These are some of the basics of life, important things . . . eat, drink, and what to wear! Yes, they are worthy of some considerable worry and effort to provide such things. There's a whole lot more implied here as well.

There's a whole lot of comfort here. Did you overlook this phrase, "and your Heavenly Father knows that you need them." God knows how important these things are! He knows you need them in order to survive in this world! He knows how much effort and work it takes to provide these things for yourself as well as for your family. Here is success in its most basic, foundational form: to be able to provide food, drink, and clothes.

Jesus is saying that IF you only seek after these things . . . you are missing the mark of living. If you seek His kingdom and His righteousness FIRST, all these things will be given to you as well. IF you get your priorities right, all the other factors of living will be given to you. In getting the number one thing right, you will experience the benefits of the right priority as well as the necessities of life. If you, on your own, pursue other priorities, you go it alone . . . but if you include God as your first priority, you will have God's help and provision and promise that all of these other things will be yours, too!

> Man is born with his hands clenched;
> he dies with them wide open. Entering life,
> he desires to grasp everything; leaving the
> world, all he possessed has slipped away.
> (Jewish Talmud)

I remind you again that to "seek first" is an ongoing process. We must come back to it on a daily basis. We are to seek and to keep on seeking every day, in every situation, in every circumstance. I come back to establishing and reinforcing this choice of priorities in life. Things change, circumstances change, people change, relationships change, we change . . . therefore the need to do this on an ongoing basis. But to get it right and keep it right will open all kinds of wonderful possibilities in living.

There was a simple, wonderful positive thinking French woman who lived in the Louisiana Bayou country. She loved it and she loved the pace of life about her, but she was surrounded by a whole bunch of negative thinking neighbors who constantly complained about "living way out here in the desolate back country."

One day, she had heard enough and she replied: "You live on the bayou, the bayou connects to the stream, the stream is connected to the river, the river flows to the gulf, the gulf flows to the ocean, and the ocean touches all the shores of the world. YOU CAN GO ANYWHERE FROM WHERE YOU ARE!" Right on! Get your number one priority right and you can go anywhere from where you are! The possibilities are endless . . . but get it right first, then all of living will flow through the filter of Matthew 6:33! That truth does not stand alone.

> HE is the image of the invisible God,
> the firstborn over all creation. For by Him
> all things were created: things in heaven
> and on earth, visible and invisible, whether
> thrones or powers or rulers or authorities;

ALL THINGS WERE CREATED BY HIM AND
FOR HIM. HE IS BEFORE ALL THINGS, AND
IN HIM ALL THINGS HOLD TOGETHER!
(Col. 1:15-17, emphasis added).

Do you have good health? Do you have a wonderful
family? Do you have a good job? Do you have a nice
salary? Do you experience success? Do you have a good
mind? If so, it all eventually can be traced back to HIM!
He is the first. He is Lord! He is supreme! He holds all of
life together . . . whether you are willing to make Him
number one or not, it doesn't change this truth! It's all
His anyhow. It's the matter of deciding who will call the
shots in life for you.

Paderewski, the great pianist, had just finished one
of his stellar performances in Carnegie Hall when he was
approached by a fan who said, "I'd give my life to play
like that."

To which the brilliant pianist sobered and replied, "I
did!"

When setting your life priorities, your "won't power"
is equally as important as your "willpower." Why? Because discipline involves choices. When you say "yes" to
something you also say "no" to a whole lot of other things.
These things to which you say no may be wonderful and
good but are they the best? Every prize in life has its
price. Every achievement has a cost that goes with it.
There is a tendency that people have when observing
any successful accomplishment of others to attribute it to
brains, brawn, talent, or lucky breaks because that lets
them off the hook. In reality, tough choices are the driving forces behind success.

Paul the Apostle lived by this principle of setting priorities and then living by them. Here is his personal testimony as his life was about to wind up: "BUT ONE THING
I DO!" In this decision there is the implication of his having said "no" to lots of things in life. The "no" that is said

to distractions will lead to the "yes" of accomplishment.

Igor Gorin, the noted Ukrainian-American baritone tells of his earlier days when he began studying voice. He loved to smoke a pipe. One day his voice instructor said to him, "Igor, you will have to make up your mind whether you are going to be a great singer or a great pipe smoker. You cannot be both!" So the choice was made . . . the pipe went.

This making of choices and setting priorities is a matter of discipline. Disciplined people tend to be happier people because they are making the best of themselves and the life choices presented to them. They are fulfilling the potential in themselves. It makes no difference what field of endeavor you are in, the best possible outcome can only be attained by exercising the discipline to make the choice. Once you have set your first priority . . . all the other choices will flow out of this one.

> If any of us would be transported to heaven for even a five-minute visit, we would never be the same after our return to earth. For the first time, we would have a true perspective on the frailty and brevity of life on earth and the absurdity of giving our hearts to things that will not last. (Ken Boa)

There is one incident set in the Ravensbruck concentration camp where 92,000 women and children died during World War II that we'll take a look at. It was a Good Friday and a group of women were lined up for the gas chamber. One of them became frantic, hysterical. From the crowd of other women not chosen for death that day, a lone figure emerged and approached the woman broken by fear and hysteria and calmly said to her: "It's all right. It's all right. I'll take your place."

That woman was Elizabeth Pilenko. She came from a

very wealthy family in the south of Russia and eventually by her choice became a nun and worked among the poor. During the war, her convent became a haven for escaping Jews. When the Gestapo came to the convent, Mother Maria (as Elizabeth Pilenko was called) was arrested and sent to Ravensbruck. There she made a lasting impression and even the guards spoke of her as "that wonderful Russian nun."

Maybe we can't quite understand how one human being can go up to another who is condemned to die and say, calmly, "Don't be afraid, I will take your place in line." In line with the rest, Mother Maria entered the gas chamber. How is such a choice made possible? Because earlier in her life she had made the ultimate choice, she had been able to seek FIRST the kingdom of God and His righteousness. Therefore every other decision and choice was filtered through that single, meaningful, ultimate choice. The decision to die was easy because earlier she had made the FIRST choice.

The choice of your priorities will determine at what level you will achieve true success! Your life is precious, but you only have the opportunity to spend it once. You can only live it in the fast-forward mode. If you have made the wrong choice previously, you can correct it and begin it all over again this time with your priorities right.

I hope the point has been made. Now we come to the final question to be asked about your priorities . . .

WHAT IS THE "FIRST" PRIORITY OF YOUR LIFE?

Chapter 8

True Success and the Self-Discipline Principle

Character will not reach its best until it is controlled, harnessed, and disciplined!

Steve Tran of Westminster, California, according to the *Arizona Republic*, closed the door on 25 activated bug bombs. He thought he had seen the last of the cockroaches that shared his apartment. When the spray reached the pilot light of the kitchen stove it ignited, blasted his front door across the street, broke all his windows, and set the furniture ablaze!

"I really wanted to kill all of them," he said. "I thought if I used a lot more, it would last longer. I had had it with bugs!" According to the label, just two canisters of the fumigant were called for. The blast caused more than $10,000 in damages to his apartment building. And the cockroaches? Tran reported, "By Sunday, I saw them walking around the apartment again!"[7]

A fool gives full vent to his anger, but
a wise man keeps himself under control
(Prov. 29:11).

The Greeks, of course, have a word for self-discipline . . . "enkrateia" which describes "the mastery of all fleshly appetites." This is a rare biblical word but was highly prized in Greek moral philosophy. For our understanding it is self-discipline, self-control, will power, composure, mental balance, firmness, stability, patience, and temperance.

I cannot tell you the source of this supposedly true story . . . possibly one of those special "Paul Harvey" stories:

It happened in a busy Nebraska town. A little old lady sedately tooled her Lincoln Town Car to the downtown post office and was looking for a place to park. As she circled, she found one right in front of the post office steps. She slowly pulled up to parallel park, when a young man in a little red, nimble sports car pulled into her spot from behind.

She rolled down her window and yelled at him, "Why did you take my parking place?"

He happily retorted, as he bounced up the steps, "Because I'm young and quick," and skipped on through the front door.

When he returned . . . she was backing her Lincoln into the side of his beautiful red sports car . . . forward and back, crash! She had trashed it pretty good by now and he came yelling down the steps for her to stop and at her driver-side window, shouted at her, "Why are you doing that?"

With a polite smile, she replied, "Because I'm old and rich!"

You've heard it said: "Begun is half-done." But I've always wondered about the other half. Perhaps, for you, in the pursuit of true success, the toughest problem is the task of disciplining yourself to keep going when things are not working as expected, when problems arise, and frustrations flood your life.

> ### NOTHING OF VALUE HAPPENS
> ### WITHOUT SELF-DISCIPLINE!

and . . .

> ### ONLY SELF-DISCIPLINE CAN TAKE YOU TO
> ### THE TOP OF THE LADDER OF SUCCESS!

Everything I have written in this book so far is extremely important for all of us who are interested in experiencing true success. We have talked about a number of principles . . . all of which are vital. But using all these concepts will not allow you to experience all the success God would desire for you to have. It's only in the application of self-discipline that it will happen. We are doing more than talking theory . . . we are challenging you to action. And self-control and self-discipline are the character traits that make for fulfillment.

A young violinist dashed up to a New York cabby, violin case in hand, and breathlessly shouted, "Quick! How do I get to Carnegie Hall?"

The cabby eyed him and the violin case and responded, "Practice, young man, practice." He could as easily have said, "Discipline, young man, discipline yourself to practice."

Where are you headed? Where is your Carnegie Hall? What is your Carnegie Hall?

It's sad to contemplate . . . but some of the most talented musicians in this world will never be heard, some of the most talented writers will never be read, some of the most talented athletes will never make the team, some of the most gifted inventors will never invent, some of the most exciting speakers will never speak in public!

Why? Because these people have never disciplined themselves enough to develop their giftedness into a quality
performance. These are the people always looking for a
short cut, the painless way to excellence, because they
believe they can deliver without paying the price.

> ## YOU CANNOT EXPERIENCE TRUE
> ## SUCCESS WITHOUT SELF-DISCIPLINE!

Real success, true success, God's success, is not in
the lucky bounce or the big break or simply being in the
right place at the right time. It is a result of disciplined
perseverance and daily effort. Maybe you have seen these
findings taken from the National Sales Executives Asso-
ciation concerning persistence:

- 80 percent of all new sales are made after the fifth call on the same prospect!

- 48 percent of all salespersons make only
  one call, then cross off the prospect.

- 25 percent quit after the second call.

- 12 percent of all sales representatives call
  three times, then quit.

- 10 percent keep calling until they succeed!

And that's how you get to be one of those special,
elite salespeople . . . the 10 percent who are disciplined
enough to continue until they succeed, who persist until
they reach their goal.

How is it possible to develop discipline in your life?
Developing new habits of self-discipline is a learning process like we learn just about everything else: observation, imitation, and repetition.

1. OBSERVATION: Good habits are learned just like

bad habits are learned behavior. Lots of harmful habits such as self-criticism, laziness, depression, tardiness, pessimism, and over-indulgence are learned and developed into character traits through relentless practice.

In the same way . . . the helpful, positive, successful habits of self-control, dedication, enthusiasm, reliability, proper nutritional habits, and substance avoidance are also learned behaviors. These have been observed somewhere, internalized, and retained through constant, continuing practice. IT IS FAR EASIER TO START DOING SOMETHING NEW THAN IT IS TO STOP DOING SOMETHING THAT IS ALREADY AN ENTRENCHED HABIT.

Well . . . who do we observe? Let's start with the lifestyle pattern lived out before us in the person of Jesus Christ, which is discovered by reading the Word of God. Suppose you need to develop the character trait of thankfulness. You can observe this in written form stated this way: "Give thanks in all circumstances, for this is God's will for you in Christ Jesus" (1 Thess. 5:18). Is this one of your habits? Should it be? If your answer is in the affirmative, then memorize this, internalize this, picture this as the habit which will replace the old habit of griping and complaining about life.

Too many people are dealing with the three "G's" of a lousy attitude: griping, gossiping, and grumbling.

A man consulting his psychiatrist complained: "Doc, I've been misbehaving, and my conscience is really bothering me."

The doctor replied, "And you want something that will strengthen your will-power and self-discipline?"

The man replied, "Well, no . . . not exactly. I was thinking of something that would weaken my conscience."

Bad habits are not broken . . . they are replaced with positive, good ones. Self-discipline is an inside job — what is on the inside will be evident in your actions.

2. IMITATION: This is a strong biblical lifestyle prin-

ciple: "Follow my example as I follow the example of Christ" (1 Cor. 11:1). This was written by Paul, who is one of the most wholesome, exciting people to imitate. He got it right.

I trust that you'll agree with me on this point — that anyone who has ever achieved anything approaching success must give a lot of credit to practice. We are constantly practicing . . . either good or bad habits.

Why do athletes spend precious time practicing? Every four years we are treated to the Olympics in which we can observe superbly trained athletes in competition. But are you aware of how many hours of practicing it takes to reach such a level of competition? Studies indicate that, on average, it takes about 10,000 hours of practice to develop a world-class athlete! The secret of winning is practicing flawless, correct techniques that have been learned from a coach or mentor who has a proven track record of success. You do not want to have a coach who has never won an event, if you can help it. Right?

3. REPETITION: In a study, it was shown that it took at least 20 repetitions before any action would become habit. Twenty reps! Twenty choices! Twenty times to think about a conscious effort. To learn a new discipline, use the same method. At first the action may seem to be dis-jointed and uncoordinated . . . but persistence will eventually achieve enough proficiency to make it a habit, good or bad. So to unlearn, re-learn, or replace a bad habit, think in terms of the longer picture — 20 times of repetition.

Even Jesus Christ repeated actions until they became habits. "He [Jesus] went to Nazareth, where He had been brought up, and on the Sabbath day He went into the synagogue AS WAS HIS CUSTOM [habit]" (Luke 4:16, emphasis added). He had been forming this habit until attending the synagogue on the Sabbath became a custom, an action done without thinking.

You can't simply erase your poor habits, but you can

override them with new thoughts and habits that are continually repeated until they become new dominant thoughts and habits — your new magnificent obsession.

Henri Matisse was 28 years younger than Auguste Renoir. The two great artists were dear friends and frequently spent time together. When Renoir was confined to his home during the last ten years of his life, Matisse visited him daily. Renoir, now almost paralyzed by arthritis, continued to paint in spite of his infirmities. One day as Matisse watched the elder painter working in his studio, fighting pain with each brush stroke, he blurted out, "Auguste, why do you continue to paint when you are in such agony?"

To which Renoir answered simply, "The beauty remains; the pain passes." The pain is lost in the victory! There you have the simple keys to building a new habit of self-discipline: observation, imitation, and repetition!

As a child, Mary Groda did not learn to read and write. Experts labeled her retarded. As an adolescent, she "earned" an additional label, "incorrigible," and was sentenced to two years in a reformatory. It was here, ironically, in this closed-in place, that Mary . . . bending to the challenge to learn . . . worked at her task for as long as 16 hours a day. Her hard work paid off: she was awarded her (GED) high school diploma.

But more misfortune was to visit Mary Groda. After leaving the reformatory, she became pregnant without the benefit of marriage. Then, two years later a second pregnancy resulted in a stroke, erasing her hard-earned powers of reading and writing. With the help and support of her father, Mary battled back, regaining what she had lost. In dire financial straits, Mary went on welfare. Finally, to make ends meet, she took in seven foster children. It was during this period that she started taking courses at a community college. Upon completion of her course work, she applied to and was accepted by the

Albany Medical School to study medicine.

In the spring of 1984 in Oregon, Mary Groda Lewis
. . . she's married now . . . paraded in full academic rega-
lia across the graduation stage. No one can know what
private thoughts went through Mary's mind as she
reached out to grasp this eloquent testimony to her self-
belief and perseverance. Her diploma announced to all
the world: Here stands on this small point of Planet Earth
a person who dared to dream the impossible dream. Here
stands Mary Groda Lewis, M.D.![8]

How did you do it, Mary? I think I can hear her reply:
"I learned self-control and self-discipline, I observed, I
imitated, and I kept at it until these goals were mine
through repetition." Mary . . . Mary, can anybody learn
these secrets of self-discipline? Anybody? "YES!"

> Dear Friends, this is now my second
> letter to you. I have written both of them
> as reminders to stimulate you to whole-
> some thinking (2 Pet. 3:1).

And to you, Peter, we address the next question:
"What is the bottom line in regards to putting self-discipline into our living?"

> For a man [person] is a slave to what-
> ever has mastered him (2 Pet. 2:19).

So the choice is quite simple . . . either develop the
good habits of success and become their slave or develop the bad habits of failure and become their slave! In
reality, these are the only two choices! There is no neu-
tral ground. And without self-discipline . . . true success
is an impossibility!

Chapter 9

True Success and the Overcoming Principle

When you can think of yesterday without
regret and of tomorrow without fear . . .
you are well on the road to success!

You cannot be on the search for success for very long without coming to the conclusion that a lifestyle without destructive emotions is a necessity. When we look at people, we can easily see them . . . part animal, part sinner, part saint, and part divine. And unless a person learns to control the destructive forces of life, there is no way to release the full power of a truly successful life. Here's the modern-day dilemma:

> THE GOOD THAT I WOULD DO . . . I DO NOT,
> THE EVIL THAT I WOULD NOT DO . . . THAT I DO.

What a wretch I am . . . who or what can deliver me from these destructive forces that would cause me to go down in defeat, cause me to live in failure and not in

113

success? One of the major reasons that you may not be doing the right thing, living the right way, is that you have not established the right habits of living.

Okay . . . so what are some of these destructive forces that prevent us from becoming the truly successful person we can be? This list is not complete . . . but it's a start: self-centeredness, envy, jealousy, resentment, hate, worry, over-sensitivity, guilt, fear, sorrow, anger, bitterness, desire for approval, frustration, and rage. Not a pretty list. Ugly all. There is a direct relationship between the influence of emotional stress on the human body and the problems as well as diseases which can be caused or aggravated by such wrongful emotions. An upset mind equals an upset body and a much lowered quality of life.

Benedict Arnold's daring, successful attack at Fort Ticonderoga proved him to be one of the most enterprising and successful generals during our Revolutionary War. He possessed many of the outstanding characteristics of a successful leader. But he also had many of the faults that have caused many a gifted person to falter and fail in later life. He was a man of great capacities, many interests, and had great stamina. He possessed initiative and a huge amount of personal drive. He was also very selfish and self-centered. And too often, where his personal interests were involved, his actions were based on emotion rather than reason.

Because he was a fighting general, he was highly esteemed by the men under his command. But members of Congress and other higher Army officers who associated with him found him to be quite a problem. His arrogance, unreasonable demands, impatience, and stubbornness made him very difficult to get along with. When he was deprived of his command in 1777, he was deeply hurt and insulted. However, when the British attacked on October 7, Arnold rallied the Revolutionary forces without any vested authority. His leadership, enthusiasm, and fighting ability once more won an important victory and Congress showed its appreciation by making him a major general.

A woman is often the greatest influencing factor in determining a man's eventual success or failure. It was in 1779 that Benedict Arnold married the 18-year-old daughter of a Tory. It is significant that in the spring of that year he first offered his services to the enemy. In May of 1780, Arnold asked for the command of West Point and he got it. He immediately informed the British that he would turn the fort over to them for 20,000 pounds sterling.

His motives for treason were personal, not political. Arnold, like any other person who becomes a traitor to others or to their own person, rationalized his actions. He, like any other disloyal person, acted on a negative self-motivator: WHAT'S IN IT FOR ME? He was betrayed from within by the destructive forces which were allowed to grow and mature until they consumed his living. Like Benedict Arnold, an outward success may become the next failure unless there is an overcoming of the destructive forces within.

Long centuries before modern day psychiatry and psychology discovered that carnal emotions are important factors in the many failures and corroding diseases of the mind and body, the Bible condemned these emotions and provided a positive cure for them.

> The acts of the sinful nature are obvious: sexual immorality, impurity and debauchery; idolatry and witchcraft; hatred, discord, jealousy, fits of rage, selfish ambition, dissensions, factions and envy; drunkenness, orgies, and the like. I warn you, as I did before, that those who live like this will not inherit the kingdom of God (Gal. 5:19-21).

Dr. William Sadler, who was impressed with the close connection between the sinful activities of the lower nature and many debilitating diseases, wrote: "No one can appreciate so fully as a doctor the amazingly large percentage of human disease and suffering which is directly traceable to worry, fear, conflict, immorality, dissipation, and ignorance . . . to unwholesome thinking and unclean living. The sincere acceptance of the principles and teachings of Christ with respect to the life of mental peace and joy, the life of unselfish thought and clean living, would at once wipe out more than half the difficulties, diseases, and sorrows of the human race!

> The teachings of Jesus applied to our modern civilization . . . understandingly applied, not merely nominally accepted . . . would so purify, uplift, and vitalize us that the race would immediately stand out as a new order of beings, possessing superior mental power and increased moral force. Irrespective of the future rewards of living, laying aside all discussion of future life, it would pay any man or woman to live the Christ-life just for the mental and moral rewards it affords here in this present world.[9]

We can even appeal to Shakespeare on this subject. In his writings, obviously, he knew enough of the Bible and human frailties to recognize that people can become sick from guilt. It was the memory of the murder of Duncan that produced those psychosomatic overtones in Lady Macbeth. Let's look at the scene when Macbeth asked the doctor about her illness and he replied:

> No so sick, my lord,
> As she is troubled with thick-coming fancies,

That keep her from her rest.

The doctor was then asked the very same question that a lot of people put to many a doctor of today:

Canst thou not minister to mind diseas'd,

Pluck from the memory a rooted sorrow,

Raze out the written troubles of the brain,

And with some sweet oblivious antidote

Cleanse the stuff'd bosom of that perilous stuff

Which weighs upon the heart?[10]

It's well documented, that we already know, that what a person eats is not nearly as important as the bitter spirit, the hatreds, the emotions, and the feelings of guilt that eat away at the insides of a person. It will take a whole lot more than a dose of baking soda, or an Alka Seltzer in the stomach to reach those acids that destroy body, mind, soul, and spirit, as well as any honest attempts at experiencing success in life. The Bible doesn't merely treat these disease-producing factors of envy, self-centeredness, resentment, hatred, and wrong living . . . it goes to the cause, to the core, with the antidote:

But the fruit of the Spirit is love, joy, peace, patience, kindness, goodness, faithfulness, gentleness and self-control. Against such things there is no law. Those who belong to Christ Jesus have crucified the sinful nature with its passions and desires (Gal. 5:22-24).

How can all of these destructive things be changed?

How can they be overcome? Let's take a bit of a time-out and consider how the human mind works. You have noticed from your own experiences that every time you are confronted with a new environment or before you do something you have never done before that there is an awareness, fear, or uneasiness that might make you hesitate before you take an action. Right? This is particularly true when you are first tempted to do a wrong action. Maybe . . . the fear has been strong enough to stop you from doing the undesirable action. This is one of the ways in which we are protected against unknown danger.

And that is why we know for a certainty that NO ONE commits any serious, wrongful deeds without stopping to think, to pause, to consider, unless the habit has already been established by previous actions of a more minor nature. It just doesn't happen in a vacuum.

No one, NOBODY, acts except in response to suggestion, self-suggestion, or auto-suggestion. Read on . . . I'll explain what I mean with some simple definitions.

SUGGESTION deals with anything you can see, hear, feel, taste, or smell. These are suggestions from the outside. How does a child learn to walk or talk? The child learns because of hearing and seeing parents walk and talk. Later . . . these suggestions can come from any outside influence such as reading from a book, watching TV, listening to a CD. Suggestion can be from a friend or a situation. It's an outside influence, good or bad, which suggests a particular action is to be taken or learned.

SELF-SUGGESTION is the suggestion you purposely give to yourself. Such take the form of thinking, seeing, hearing, feeling, tasting, and smelling through the power of your self-imagination or self-suggestion. You can picture the word symbols, or you can say the words to yourself, or you can write them down, or you can visualize the action you want to take. This is also what you do when you learn any kind of a self-motivator. It is thinking the thought, making the statement, seeing the picture. It is a self-suggestion, generated from within, based on the input you have programmed into your thinking.

You have heard of the term used in computer programming: "GIGO." In other words, "garbage in equals garbage out." It works as a negative or positive . . . depending on the input.

AUTO-SUGGESTION is just what the name implies, an automatic suggestion. It is the suggestion from the subconscious mind that flashes to the conscious in the form of an image of seeing, hearing, feeling, tasting, smelling, or word symbols. It can also be taught.

Consider this example. Johnny enters a new high school as a freshman . . . along with lots of other new students. Naturally he wants to make friends and he does. Some of his new friends half-jokingly and half-seriously suggest that they go out to the "midnight auto parts" place. They were planning on stealing accessories or wheels or what-have-you from cars. This is a suggestion, a temptation.

Johnny's conscience will bother him at this point . . . unless he has already developed the habit of stealing. BUT, if Johnny's parents have taught him such self-motivators as "Thou shalt not steal" or "Have the courage to say 'no' " . . . these will flash from his subconscious mind into his conscious mind as a preventive. This is auto-suggestion at work.

If this input has been successful and a previous practice, Johnny will exercise the courage to say "no" and he may even use his influence to motivate his new-found friends to also do the right thing because it is right.

This is powerful training and a preventive against wrong actions and wrong thoughts. Suggestion comes out of the environment, self-suggestion comes from within, and auto-suggestion comes from good teaching, good repetitive habits of thought, because out of the heart will flow the issues of life.

Here is how important such practices are and how they are to be passed on to the next generation:

> Fix these words of mine in your hearts and minds; tie them as symbols on your hands and bind them on your foreheads. Teach them to your children, talking about them when you sit at home and when you walk along the road, when you lie down and when you get up. Write them on the doorframes of your houses and on your gates, so that your days and the days of your children may be many in the land that the Lord swore to give your forefathers . . . if you carefully observe all these commands I am giving you to follow . . . to love the Lord your God, to walk in all His ways and to hold fast to Him . . . then the Lord will . . . (Deut. 11:18-23).

The promises go on and on of what will be a very positive lifestyle for all of God's people who are obedient in these areas of living. He promises them a lifetime of success based on the positive inputs of His concepts, His words, and His principles so that they guide and control the actions of living.

If you read further on in this biblical chapter you discover that God had presented them a choice of enjoying His blessings or enduring a curse. The blessings would come with obedience, the curse would follow their disobedience to the commands and words of God. The bottom line in this passage carries with it one last admonition, "Be sure that you obey all the decrees and laws I am setting before you today" (Deut. 11:32). It's a piece of advice which still holds true for today. Upon what life concepts will you build your life in order to experience real, true success? Your own? Concepts from this worldly system? Or life principles based on the eternal, true successful words of God?

So, we've worked our way together to this point . . . now what do we do about the destructive kinds of emotions which can rob us of success in so many ways. Such things left unchecked and undealt with are like walking through life on top of land mines ready to explode without warning. How do we rid ourselves of such problems? Is there an answer which can help in overcoming such emotions? Here are a few principles which I believe will help you. But if you find that in your life these do not yield easily or quickly . . . you may need to go for some competent help, a counselor, psychologist, a trusted friend, or a loving pastor.

Taking on some of these destructive forces in our life is much like fighting giants. Now the Bible again has the answers we need. The story is familiar to anyone who has ever read the Bible or attended Sunday school or church — David and Goliath. Let's move on to some . . .

BIBLICAL PRINCIPLES FOR FIGHTING GIANTS

1. WE PREPARE TO FIGHT GIANTS IN SECRET PLACES. Life battles are won or lost in secret closets, in wilderness places, in out-of-the-way places. We become the persons we in actuality are when we are alone. Sloppy, careless life or spiritual disciplines can't be made up in the battle, it's too late, then.

You cannot possibly wait until the moment of temptation, the moment of decision, the moment of the contest, the moment of adversity to decide to do battle with your giants. David was ready for the public encounter with his giant because in private, behind the scenes, all alone with himself, his sling, his harp, and his God, he became the man in private before he became the man in public. He knew how his slingshot worked because of practice. His was a religion of reality because he knew how it worked. His was not a religion of theory. Here, where nobody can see what goes on, is where the battles are fought for principle and integrity.

2. GIANTS WILL KEEP COMING. In this story, Goliath kept coming day after day, twice a day to taunt and flaunt, to take captive and place in bondage. When we have battled one giant, we soon discover that there is another to take his place. Often a giant can return for a re-match. But, then too, giants have other giants to whom they are related. You don't just fight one battle and then settle down to living without inner conflict for the rest of your life.

In the life of David, when he was at least 78 years old, there were four more giants that needed to be conquered in his life. (Read the story in 2 Sam. 21:15-22.) The four who were listed here were all related to Goliath. The truth here is that whatever is not conquered in your youth will come back to haunt you the rest of your life.

Have you wondered why David chose five smooth stones from the brook? How about one for Goliath and the other four for his relatives. But on the day of his conflict, David didn't go far enough . . . so these four survived and had to be dealt with later in life.

3. KNOW A GIANT WHEN YOU SEE ONE. You might laugh at this one, because giants are huge and blustery and easy to spot. But as you read this story, you find that David's own brother ridiculed David and what he was about to do. Now if Eliab had said to us what he said to David, we'd have had a fight with him instead of with Goliath. Eliab was not the giant . . . he was a problem with his bad attitude. David was able to keep focused on what the most immediate and important problem was. (Read it from 1 Sam. 17:28.) We are so easily

sidetracked and thrown off focus.

4. DON'T LISTEN TO THE WRONG ADVICE. There are always people ready to give you advice and offer you another way to deal with the giants of your life. King Saul represents such people. In so many words, Saul said to David, "You're too small, you're too young, and you're not using the right methods or the right armor." When we go out to do battle with these spiritual giants, there is a right way and there is a wrong way. If David had followed Saul's advice and used his armor and his methods . . . he would have gotten the same results that Saul and his army were already experiencing: fear and bondage, being stripped naked.

Read this carefully:

> Be strong in the Lord and in His mighty power. Put on the full armor of God so that you can take your stand against the devil's schemes. For our struggle is not against flesh and blood, but against the rulers, against the authorities, against the powers of this dark world and against the spiritual forces of evil in the heavenly realms. THEREFORE PUT ON THE FULL ARMOR OF GOD (Eph. 6:10-12, emphasis added).

5. KNOW THAT FIGHTING GIANTS CAN BE INTIMIDATING. Giants are big, giants threaten us, giants are tough, giants are big talkers and we can easily become afraid. Goliath was more than nine feet tall in contrast to David, who was about normal height for a teenager. But David was not intimidated because he viewed this giant, this obstacle to obtaining victory, through the eyes of God. Say it with me, say it out loud:

GOD IS BIGGER THAN ANY GIANT IN MY LIFE!

From God's viewpoint, Goliath didn't have a remote chance of winning! You can almost begin to feel sorry for the giant. David was grossly under-matched . . . he was much too much of an opponent for Goliath to handle. David refused to be bullied, bluffed, blown away or over-whelmed by this giant. David was in control because God was in control!

6. GIANT FIGHTING IS A LONELY EXPERIENCE. David, while still a teenager, walked down into that valley and across the creek alone. Yes, God was there, but you can't always reach out a hand and touch flesh with God. There comes a point in your life when you have explored all the advice, exhausted all the counsel, enlisted all the prayer support, and used all the help you can get. Ulti-mately, you have to go out and handle, fight, face, your giant alone. It can be a lonely business, humanly speak-ing. (Read Rom. 8:31, 37-39 and Isa. 14:16-17.)

7. KNOW WHAT TO REMEMBER AND KNOW WHAT TO FORGET. We are listening in on this most interesting conversation as David spoke to Saul:

> Your servant has been keeping his father's sheep. When a lion or a bear came and carried off a sheep from the flock, I went after it, struck it and rescued the sheep from its mouth. When it turned on me, I seized it by its hair, struck it and killed it. Your servant has killed both the lion and the bear; this uncircumcised Philistine will be like one of them (1 Sam. 17:34-36).

Wow, what a scene. And just how did the killing of lion and bear take place? Apparently David did it with his bare hands. No wonder the giant didn't strike fear into his heart.

At the point of his conflict with this giant . . . David remembered the victories of his past! Not us . . . we tend to recall all the bad experiences, the times when we were defeated by a giant, all the setbacks, all the times it didn't work. The enemy of your soul, and some of your best friends, all like to remind you of things you should forget.

David recalled his triumphs! After he had killed Goliath, he took his sword, his head, and all his battle paraphernalia and put them in his tent. Some of these items were later placed in the house of the Lord. They became trophies! What do you do with a trophy? You display it. And years later, when David was again doing battle, he took the sword of Goliath and used it again in another battle. You'll need to remember past victories to help defeat another giant you may be facing today!

We have at our disposal the same weapons which David used in his battle with Goliath:

- FAITH AND TRUST IN GOD!
- A DETERMINATION TO NOT LET THE GIANT DEFEAT HIM!
- THE FORESIGHT TO PRACTICE WITH HIS WEAPONS BEFORE THE BATTLE TOOK PLACE!
- COURAGE TO NOT BE AFRAID!
- THE CORRECT PERSPECTIVE — THIS WASN'T HIS BATTLE, IT WAS GOD'S!
- CONFIDENCE IN WHO HE HAD BECOME!
- AN ATTITUDE WHICH PREDICTED A VICTORY!

There's an old adage which goes like this:

> A BRAVE PERSON DIES ONLY ONCE . . . BUT A COWARD DIES A THOUSAND TIMES!

When fear is mingled with self-preservation at the point of crisis and we panic instead of acting, in a fleeting moment we lay the basis for a lifetime of guilt. WHEN we do not pass our own test for courage, or fail to measure up to the minimum standards for what we know is right, we have unchained a giant of a ghost which prowls the cellars of our days and nights. This giant gives us no rest and peace. It unleashes a giant that does entrap us.

The French writer Albert Camus, in his book *The Fall*, paints a very frightening word picture of just such a man, haunted by a fleeting act of cowardice from out of his past. Time brings no relief. This is the story, recalled by him one rainy evening in an Amsterdam bar, where he has sought refuge from his past in company and a drink:

> He was a respected Paris lawyer, a pleader of noble causes, secure in his self-esteem, immune to judgment . . . he thought. A silent listener hears his confession of the painful moment when the ghost of his life was unchained.
>
> "That particular night in November, I was returning to the West Bank. It was past midnight, a rainy mist was falling and few people on the street. On the bridge, I passed behind a figure leaning over the railing and seeming to stare at the river. On closer view I made out a slim young woman dressed in black. I went on. I had gone some fifty yards when I heard the sound . . . a body striking the water. I turned. Almost at once I heard a cry for help, repeated several times, then it ceased. Then silence. . . . I wanted to run and yet didn't stir. I told myself I had to be quick and then an irresistible weakness

settled over me. 'Too late . . . too far,' I told myself . . . then slowly, under the rain, I went away, I informed no one."

In the last page of the book, he returns once more to this scene of this moment of cowardice in the face of necessary action and helplessly cries out into the night of his pain: "O young woman, throw yourself into the water again so that I may a second time have the chance of saving both of us!"[11]

Every day, in small, but oh-so-important ways, we prepare ourselves for that moment in life where and when we meet our giants, where we shall die once the death of courage . . . or live to die a thousand times a coward, a lost battle, a lost life! These life issues of dealing with the baggage of bondage to destructive emotions must not be put off in our mad scramble to achieve success in life. There is no way under God's heaven that you can become the real, true success you desire with the bondage of the past dragging you down. It's time to break free! It's time to face any of these giants in your life! You can do it! It will not happen in your strength alone . . . but God is the ultimate weapon to use to set you free!

James Russell put it so clearly:

> ONCE TO EVERY MAN AND NATION COMES THE MOMENT TO DECIDE, IN THE STRIFE OF TRUTH WITH FALSEHOOD, FOR THE GOOD OR EVIL SIDE; SOME GREAT CAUSE, GOD'S NEW MESSIAH, OFFERING EACH THE BLOOM OR BLIGHT, AND THE CHOICE GOES BY FOREVER, TWIXT THAT DARKNESS AND THAT LIGHT!

To experience all that real, true success has to offer

to you . . . there is a price to pay — overcoming the
giants that would keep you in bondage is one! Every prize
has a price and this is one of those prices which must be
paid in order to succeed in real freedom!

Chapter 10

True Success and the Attitude Principle

Nothing can prevent the person with a right mental attitude from achieving success . . . while nothing on earth can help the person with the wrong attitude!

Let's take a look at two different kids: The parents of the first were somewhat mismatched, to say the least. His father was unemployed with no formal schooling. His mother was a public school teacher. This child was born in Port Huron, Michigan, with an IQ estimated to be 81 (normal is 90 to 110). They had to take him out of school after the first three months, due to a bout with scarlet fever and respiratory infections, then enrolled him again two years later. He was going deaf. His emotional health was poor. He liked to play with fire and on one occasion burned down his father's barn. He showed some manual dexterity, but communicated poorly. But he did want to be a scientist or railroad mechanic.

The second child, a girl, didn't show much more early promise. She was born to an alcoholic father. As a child she was sickly, bed-ridden, often hospitalized, erratic in behavior, a nail-biter, with numerous other phobias. She also wore a back brace from a spinal defect and constantly, by her behavior, sought attention. She was also a daydreamer with no well-defined life goals. However, she did express a desire to help the elderly and the poor.

Who were these kids?

The boy from Port Huron became one of the world's greatest inventors: Thomas A. Edison. The awkward, sickly girl became a champion of the oppressed: Eleanor Roosevelt.

If we had been called upon to evaluate these two, it is likely that neither would have been voted, as children, as the most likely to succeed. What really separates people from mediocrity? Again and again, time and research has proven this to be an undefinable life quality best described as "mental attitude." What causes people — even children from the same family, with the same genes, environment, and upbringing — to go through life at totally different success levels?

Geologists tell us that only 3 percent of the earth's fresh water supply is on the surface as rivers and lakes. The other 97 percent remains underground in huge subterranean reservoirs . . . much like the hidden potential of human beings! How do we manage to tap into the hidden possibilities within? How do we bring to the surface the possibilities that God has placed in our kids, ourselves, and the people we touch and have influence upon?

Now I can't give you a definitive answer . . . but I can tell you ONE place to start! It's by cleaning up your vocabulary of three of the most malignant words any of us can utter. What are the three most malignant words we are never to use again?

"I AM ONLY. . . ."

In this case, Jerry said: "I am only a child!" It can also be translated to say, "I am only a young person!" Jerry, or Jeremiah, would later go on to become one of the greatest prophets God has ever called and used in human history. BUT . . . FIRST, God had to deal with his usage of such put-down language.

How many of us, and how many times, have we limited ourselves and what God wants to do through us by saying: "I AM ONLY A . . ."? True success does not come out of an attitude which denies God and God's creation. Real success is not born out of disparaging the human being which God has made. The excuses can be endless . . . perhaps you've used them or heard others express it like any of the following.

> I am only . . . a senior citizen.
> I am only . . . a teenager.
> I am only . . . a minority person.
> I am only . . . a handicapped person.
> I am only . . . timid.
> I am only . . . a one-talent person.
> I am only . . . afraid of success.
> I am only . . . one!
> I am only . . . little ole ME!

The *Wall Street Journal* carried the story about Harry Lipsig, who at age 88 decided to leave the New York law firm he had spent 60 years building, and open a brand new law firm. He accepted his first case and here it is:

A lady was suing the city of New York because a drunken police officer had struck and killed her 71-year-old husband with the squad car. She argued that the city had deprived her of her husband's future earnings potential. The city countered back that at age 71, he had little earnings potential. They thought they had a clever defense . . . until it dawned on them that this lady's argument about her husband's future potential was being advanced by a vigorous 88-year-old attorney! The city settled out of court for one and a quarter million. What if Harry Lipsig had said: "I am only a senior citizen"!?

Did you hear about the three guys walking on a beach when they happened upon an old lamp partially buried in the sand? They picked it up and wiped it off. A "genie" popped out and told them, "I'll grant each of you one wish."

The first man whispered, "I wish I were ten times smarter."

"You are now ten times smarter," announced this genie.

The second murmured, "I wish I were a hundred times smarter."

"You are now a hundred times smarter," the genie mandated.

The third said, "I wish I were a thousand times smarter."

The genie pointed to him and declared, "You are now a woman!"

We don't want to hear it any more — "I am only a woman" —either! Do you know that the two highest IQ scores ever recorded on an IQ test belonged to women? It may not have been intelligence or ability or competence that have held women back . . . it's those cancerous words expressed, "I am only. . . ."

Well, there is a context in which these words appear. Please read it carefully with me:

> The word of the Lord came to me, saying, "Before I formed you in the womb I knew you, before you were born I set you apart; I appointed you as a prophet to the nations."
>
> "Ah, Sovereign Lord," I said, "I do not know how to speak; I am only a child."

But the Lord said to me, "Do not say, 'I am only a child.' You must go to everyone I send you to and say whatever I command you. Do not be afraid of them, for I am with you and will rescue you," declares the Lord (Jer. 1:4-8).

And the rest is history as they say. Jeremiah went on to become one of the most successful spokespersons that God had ever chosen. A true success in every sense of the word. But first there was an attitude adjustment which God had to administer.

DOES IT EVER PLEASE GOD FOR YOU TO USE "I AM ONLY . . ." AS AN EXCUSE?

No! A thousand times . . . NO! NO! NO! This became a put-down, an excuse, a rationalization. It's not pleasing to Him — besides, in His sight, it's not even a good excuse! Don't even think of it!

WHY? Because it's an insult to God! To have one of His special, wonderfully created human beings bring into question any ability. "Before I formed you in the womb I knew you" is an absolutely awesome, mind-blowing statement. And in that special act of creation, were you shortchanged? He knew all about you! He knew you could do whatever He or life would ask of you . . . with His help. He knew of all the hidden potential placed inside of you!

Every child, every human being in this world, male or female, black or white, yellow or brown . . . should grow up knowing and believing these two things about themselves: YOU ARE LOVED AND YOU ARE CAPABLE!

What devastation to any worthwhile accomplishment is released by these words, "I am only . . ." When it's repeated, the emphasis seems to be on the "only." When the word "only" is invoked or used, you in other words, are saying "I'm alone, I'm by myself, without others or their help, there is no more, merely, simply nothing, solitary, the one and only, and without any further help coming." No wonder God rebuked Jeremiah for even saying it. To tell God that you are alone is an insult to all He has promised and provided. There may be other legitimate excuses you can use to explain why success has not been yours . . . but this particular one does not hold water or make good logic when hurled in the face of God.

I am challenging you to replace the "I am only . . ." in your vocabulary with three equally powerful motivators on the positive side:

> ## "I CAN DO!"

These three words are also from God's Word. Paul the Apostle had all the "I am only" words knocked out of him in his life until he could come to the point where he was able to say, "I can do!" There is a context to these words that is also important:

> I know what it is to be in need, and I know what it is to have plenty. I have learned the secret of being content in any and every situation, whether well fed or hungry, whether living in plenty or in want. I CAN DO EVERYTHING THROUGH HIM WHO GIVES ME STRENGTH (Phil. 4:12-13, emphasis added).

The source of all strength, the source of successful living and how to do it comes through "Him who gives me strength!"

The "I am only" expression is devastatingly destructive to the soul while the "I can do" is more positively uplifting and helpful! That's not all there is to this, God has made more, many more, wonderful plans for His children so that all of us can affirm . . .

GOD HAS A WONDERFUL, EXCITING PLAN FOR ME!

God had many plans for the life and ministry of Jeremiah but he had to first remove those deadly words which will paralyze a person into non-action, non-decision, and oblivion. These "I am only" words will short-circuit God's exciting plans for a person or a nation.

Incredible, because here hidden in the Old Testament, God lets us in on a secret. "Before you were born I set you apart!" We drop down further in this exchange to read, "See, today I appoint you over nations and king-doms to uproot and tear down, to destroy and overthrow, to build and to plant!" Great plans already in place for Jeremiah while still in the womb. Awesome!

GOD HAS AN EXCITING PLAN FOR YOU, TOO! He has placed within you a potential which you may never have recognized. Will He ever pull back the shades and let each of us see what His plan really was for our lives?

Let me tell you about two more boys. One is assisting the priest at the altar, as communion is being served. This young man happened to spill the cruet (container) of wine. The priest reached out and slapped the young man with these words, "You clumsy oaf, you will never amount to anything in this world!"

The other young man was also serving wine with another priest in New York City. He was clumsy, too, and spilled the cruet of wine as he was serving the priest. This priest reached out, with a gentle touch and a know-ing smile said, "One day, you will be greatly used in the church to help others."

Who were these two boys? The first was named Marshall Tito who became one of the worst dictators this world has ever seen. The second was named Fulton J. Sheen. So now you do know the rest of this story.

God sees potential in you that no one else has ever seen. If you believe in Him, if you believe in His plan for your life, you can accomplish more than you ever dared to dream. This is not a concept based on a single verse out of the Book. It can be seen everywhere, if you will look for it. Let's try these on for size:

> Grace and peace be yours in abundance through the knowledge of God and of Jesus our Lord. His divine power has given us everything we need for life and godliness through our knowledge of Him who called us by His own glory and goodness. Through these He has given us His very great and precious promises, so that through them YOU MAY PARTICIPATE IN THE DIVINE NATURE (2 Pet. 1:2-4, emphasis added).

> For we are God's workmanship, CREATED IN CHRIST JESUS TO DO GOOD WORKS, which God prepared in advance for us to do (Eph. 2:10, emphasis added).

"CREATED" . . . not a happening, not by luck, not some slimy blob rising out of the ooze of the unknown past but "created"! Carefully crafted, meticulously planned, created in advance to do good works!

YOU are a miracle, special and rare! YOU have been sent prophets, poets, wise men, artists, composers, preachers, teachers, and even the Son of God with a good word about who you are and what your potential really is! YOU have been told that you are the salt of this world! YOU are the light in a dark world! YOU have the secret of moving mountains placed inside of you! Instead . . . YOU have beaten your chest in anguish, cursed the darkness, and refused to accept the consequences of your thoughts and actions. YOU have searched for a scapegoat and when all else has failed, YOU have blamed God and hidden behind "but I am only . . ."!

When the Romans ruled the world as the number one power, there was one Roman general who had a unique way of dealing with any condemned spies caught and brought before him for trial. Once condemned by trial, with the condemned spy standing before him, he offered a choice: choose the execution squad or choose the "black door." So, another spy, just condemned, chooses the known quantity of the execution squad to be led out and dispatched.

As these sounds of execution carry back into the room where the general and his aide are sitting, "General," the aide asks, "what is behind the black door?"

"Freedom," the general replies, "but few men have the courage to choose the unknown, even over death."

God has plans and choices for YOU! Therefore, choose wisely! Choose to let go of all the "I am only . . . " kind of rationalizations!

> ### WHEN YOU CHOOSE, GOD WILL HELP YOU TO BECOME ALL THAT YOU CAN BE!

When you have chosen to put aside the "I am only's" in your life, He will then help you with what He has chosen for you to do. Did you notice, as we read the words from Jeremiah, exactly how much God was involved in this whole process of moving the prophet to being the person God had planned for him? I formed you . . . I knew you . . . I set you apart . . . I appointed you . . . I send you . . . I am with you . . . I will rescue you . . . I have put My words in your mouth . . . I appoint you! All of this comes out of that passage. You, as well as Jeremiah, are human becomings! Not simply human beings! YOU are capable of great things! YOUR potential is unlimited!

Who else of God's creation has mastered fire or conquered gravity or pierced the skies in flight? Who has
been able to conquer diseases? Never put yourself down.
Never settle for the crumbs of life! Never hide your talents! You have the fabulous power to choose, which the
angels in heaven don't have. Think of your life choices.

> CHOOSE to . . .
> love rather than to hate
> laugh rather than cry
> create rather than destroy
> persevere rather than quit
> to build up rather than tear down
> praise rather than gossip
> heal rather than wound
> give rather than take
> act rather than procrastinate
> grow rather than rot
> pray rather than curse
> light a lamp rather than snuff it out
> live rather than die!

CHOOSE to never say "I am only . . ." again. Let God
guide you to uncover the potential hidden within you
and follow God's plan for real success!

In a fourth grade art class, some children were working with plasticine, a clay-like substance that can be used
over and over because it doesn't harden like clay. One
girl had made a nice model of a creature with wings. The
teacher asked her to show it to the class, so she held it
up and said, "See, an angel!"

There were exclamations of delight from the class
and teacher. Then the girl quickly molded the angel into
a ball and asked, "Okay, now, what's this?" Nobody could
come up with an answer, except to say, "it's a ball."

"Nope," said the girl who was doing the molding,
"it's a hiding angel."

The next day when the children returned to their art class, they had a visitor. Another child pointed to the ball of plasticine and said to the guest, "You know what this is? It's a hiding angel."

YOU may have something very special hidden in you! Something you are about to release, with God's plan and direction. Rather than saying, "I am only . . ." how about changing the expression to this:

> I AM A CHILD OF GOD! BEFORE I WAS FORMED IN THE WOMB GOD KNEW ME. BEFORE I WAS BORN, I WAS SET APART FOR SOMETHING GOOD AND BEAUTIFUL AND EXCITING AND WONDERFUL AND MEANINGFUL AND NOBLE!

What a re-affirmation with which to start all over again, to make a fresh beginning. When you respond to God, He always responds to you. The bottom line in setting Jeremiah on the right thinking, the right attitudinal track sounds this way. What a promise!

> GET YOURSELF READY! Stand up and say to them whatever I command you. Do not be terrified by them, or I will terrify you before them. TODAY I HAVE MADE YOU A FORTIFIED CITY, AN IRON PILLAR AND A BRONZE WALL to stand against the whole land . . . they will fight against you but will NOT overcome you, FOR I AM WITH YOU AND WILL RESCUE YOU," declares the Lord (Jer. 1:17-19).

I firmly believe that God wants to use you! He wants to make you a real success in every sense of the word. But first the attitudes which have been long held must be dealt with. Yes . . . God wants you to be a successful person without guilt, which can only be done in God's way with God's Word as your guide.

Bill Mann was one of those talented, blessed people, with a great singing voice. He relates a story about the most emotionally moving concert he ever sang. It happened after the planned concert was over and he returned to his dressing room. Waiting for him was a woman who was blind, deaf, and mute. Through the lady who was with her, Annie Sullivan, she asked if he would sing for her the last song he had sung in the concert.

"Sure," Bill Mann replied. As he began to sing to this audience of one, a lady who stood about six inches away from his face, she placed her fingers on his lips and on his vocal chords. He sang it once more, "Were You There When They Crucified My Lord?"

As he finished the song, a tear trickled down the face of Helen Keller. Indistinctly, she said, as the words were repeated by Annie Sullivan, "I was there!"

Deaf, blind, and mute from birth. Too much for any person to bear up under? Well . . . no, there probably was no contemporary of hers who gave more insight into the meaning of life, suffering, or the love of God, than did Helen Keller. It would have been easy for her to say, "I am only blind, deaf, and mute."

TODAY . . . will you allow the Spirit of God, the words of God, to touch your life, lips, soul, spirit, and mind until the words, "I am only" will be taken from your life? And . . . replace "I AM ONLY . . ." with

> ### "I AM A CHILD OF GOD!"

and

> ### "I CAN DO ALL THINGS THROUGH CHRIST WHO GIVES ME STRENGTH!"

Chapter 11

True Success and the Gratitude Principle

*Gratitude is not only the greatest
of virtues . . . it is also the parent
of all the others.*

The colorful 19th century showman and gifted violinist Nicolo Paganini was playing a difficult piece before a packed house. A full orchestra surrounded him . . . then, in the middle of a difficult section of music, one string snapped and hung down from his instrument. Beads of perspiration popped out on his forehead. He frowned but continued to play, improvising!

To the conductor's surprise, a second string broke . . . then a third! Now there were three limp strings dangling from Paganini's violin as this master performer completed the difficult composition on the one string. The audience jumped to its feet in good Italian fashion, filled the hall with shouts and screams, "Bravo! Bravo!" As the applause died down, the violinist asked the people to sit back down. Even though they knew there was no way they could expect an encore, they sat down.

He held the violin high for all to see. He nodded at

the conductor to begin the encore, then turned to the crowd and with a twinkle in his eye, smiled and shouted, "Paganini . . . and one string!" After that announcement he played the single-stringed Stradivarius, held beneath his chin and played the final piece on ONE string as the audience and conductor shook their heads in amazement. "Paganini and one string!" And he finished the piece to thunderous applause!

What an attitude of fortitude. I don't think this will surprise you very much . . . but I believe the most important decision that you or I can make on a day-to-day basis is our choice of attitude. An attitude of gratitude is that single string which keeps us going or hinders our lifestyle progress. When the attitude of gratitude is right . . . there will be no mountain too high, no valley too deep, no night too dark, no dream too far out, or no challenge too great!

There are lots of things in this life that make an attitude of gratitude tough to maintain. Have you read "Murphy" lately? I am talking about the Murphy of "Murphy's Laws" fame, the "if-anything-can-go-wrong-it-will-at-the-most-unexpected-time" Murphy. According to him and some of his laws:

> A day without a crisis is a total loss.
> The other line always moves faster.
> 90 percent of everything is crud.
> Whatever hits the fan will not be evenly
>   distributed.
> The repairman will have never seen a model
>   like ours before.
> Friends come and go but enemies accumulate.
> Beauty is only skin deep but ugly goes clear
>   to the bone.

Talk about attitude assassinators! Yes, they happen, maybe. But to adopt such an attitude about life and success will only make you more pessimistic. I suspect that things didn't always go right back in the days of Paul. How did he become the optimistic person as expressed in what he wrote? Did he never have to put up with days like we do?

> Speak to one another with psalms, hymns and spiritual songs. SING AND MAKE MUSIC IN YOUR HEART to the Lord, always giving thanks to God the Father for EVERYTHING, in the name of our Lord Jesus Christ (Eph. 5:19-20, emphasis added).

> And whatever you do, whether in word or deed, do it all in the name of the Lord Jesus, GIVING THANKS to God the Father through Him (Col. 3:17, emphasis added).

> Be joyful always; pray continually; GIVE THANKS IN ALL CIRCUMSTANCES, for this is God's will for you in Christ Jesus (1 Thess. 5:16-18, emphasis added).

> Do not be anxious about anything, but in everything, by prayer and petition, WITH THANKSGIVING, present your requests to God. And the peace of God, which transcends all understanding, will guard your hearts and minds in Christ Jesus (Phil. 4:6-7, emphasis added).

Did you catch the relationship? There's the mention of "mind" and "thanksgiving." We have tended to overload our minds with crud, garbage, and excess baggage which needs to be jettisoned to be replaced with the attitude of gratitude. There needs to be a re-thinking process so that we can concentrate on rejoicing and giving thanks.

There is another problem with maintaining the single string of gratitude, and it's called "blame." It's such a human foible to always be on the lookout for a scapegoat, someone or something to blame. It's the shifting of responsibility from ourselves to some outside influence. But if this is done often and becomes a habit it takes root and flowers into full-blown cynicism. What an enemy of success placing blame can be. It's a fruitless exercise which only adds to the burden of life.

Blame never affirms anybody, it assaults.
Blame never restores anybody, it wounds.
Blame never solves anything, it complicates.
Blame never brings us together, it separates.
Blame never has a smile, it frowns.
Blame never offers forgiveness, it rejects.
Blame never builds up, it destroys.
Blame never gives anything positive, it takes.
Blame never is certain, it doubts.
Blame never lifts up another, it downs.

CONSIDER GRATITUDE AS A CELEBRATION!

Pastor Mark Rutland relates the following: Some years ago I came in contact with a teenager who had been raised by his grandparents from his infancy. The boy's father had been killed in an auto accident and then his mother just disappeared. The grandparents had been doing all they knew how to do for him at great sacrifice. It's a tough assignment for anyone to raise a teenager while in their sixties and seventies. Nobody should have to go through that twice.

For several years this teen had rewarded them with unfathomable rebellion, anger, and sin. He made that old couple miserable. Finally, as his pastor, I could not stand it. I took him aside and said, "Remember when they took you in? You could have gone to an orphanage. You could have been a ward of the court. Your mother disappeared, your father is dead, and these kind people, your grandparents, took you in. They got up with you in the middle of the night. They changed your diapers, fed you, and clothed you. They raised you at sacrifice to themselves. Nobody would have blamed them if they had said, 'We just can't handle it at our age.' "

He replied, bitterly, "Do you think this is the first time I've ever thought of all that? I know what they've done. But what am I supposed to do . . . spend the rest of my life saying 'Thank you'?"

Well . . . as a matter of fact, YES! Everybody should! Life is to be an expression of gratitude to God, to others, to people who have given to us! Yes, we are to spend the rest of this life being grateful, offering thanksgiving, and saying it to God and to others!

There are lots of ways in which this could be done. Synonyms for "gratitude" include: gratefulness, appreciation, thankfulness, thanks, acknowledgment, recognition, obligation, and thanksgiving. Is there a clue here for us?

There is one man who had learned how to make the offering of thanks almost like an art form. He was declared to be a man after God's own heart . . . and I happen to believe this was one of the reasons — his habit of living in thanksgiving. He had learned the blessings and benefits of living a thankful life.

> Shout for joy to the Lord, all the earth.
> Worship the Lord with gladness; come
> before Him with joyful songs.
> Know that the Lord is God.
> It is He who made us, and we are His;
> we are His people, the sheep of His
> pasture.

> Enter His gates with thanksgiving and
> His courts with praise; give thanks to Him
> and praise His name.
>
> For the Lord is good and His love en-
> dures forever;
>
> His faithfulness continues through all
> generations (Ps. 100).

This habit of King David was not a once-in-a-while thing to do. Obviously it became a lifestyle of his, an ongoing habit. In fact, he made it a forever kind of thing to do.

> You turned my wailing into dancing;
> you removed my sackcloth and clothed me
> with joy, that my heart may sing to you
> and not be silent. O Lord my God, I will
> give you thanks forever (Ps. 30:11-12).

That attitude can easily be contrasted to the attitude of a former great civilization which the apostle Paul points out as a failure. He traces their demise and a root cause of their failure to the lack of this attitude.

> For although they knew God, they nei-
> ther glorified him as God nor gave thanks
> to Him, but their thinking became futile and
> their foolish hearts were darkened" (Rom.
> 1:21). (You can read the entire context from
> Rom. 1:18-31.)

What a contrast. A major concern in our quest for success in living is that we also learn how to develop a grateful attitude. The grateful person is the person who sees others and the hand of God in the goodness and successes of life that have come their way. And in the very bottom-line living of life . . . we really have nothing, we are nothing, except what has been given to us by way of heritage, and the goodness, mercy, and grace of a loving God. Without Him we never would have come into existence, without Him we cannot long sustain our existence. There is no such a thing as a completely "self-made" man or woman. We are the product of so much and so many who have gone before and are going with us, enabling us in the present.

To the grateful person . . . all of living becomes an adventure. And the more we learn how to develop the gratitude-attitude, the more enjoyable life becomes!

> **THE PERSON WHO FORGETS THE LANGUAGE OF GRATITUDE WILL NEVER BE ON SPEAKING TERMS WITH HAPPINESS!**

WHY SHOULD GRATITUDE BE AN ATTITUDE TO CULTIVATE?

Homer Smith is an itinerant black carpenter from the southern part of these United States. He's written a number of books and among them is *The Lilies of The Field*, in which one of the main characters is a German-Roman Catholic Mother Superior who is shepherding a group of four or five nuns in the desert of New Mexico. Hoping to build a church there in the desert, this curmudgeon of an old nun is working her fingers to the bone and praying that God will send her a way to get her chapel built.

When Homer Smith drives up in his battered station wagon, she is convinced he is that instrument of God sent to her in answer to her prayers. This crotchety old German nun badgers, cajoles, coaxes, and tricks Homer Smith into staying and building that church.

Despite all his efforts and the chapel being built, she will NOT tell Homer "Thank you." No way, no how! Near the end of the book, by the use of an English lesson, Homer is able to trick that curmudgeon of a nun into

saying, "Thank you" for the very first time in her life to
anyone. When she does, she finds it a jolting experience!
You just need to read the book for the rest of the story.
You will enjoy it.

Why be grateful? The essence is captured with the
words, "I am obligated." We reject that kind of thinking,
after all, who wants to be obligated. Sorry, but that's the
way it is. "I am obligated both to Greeks and non-Greeks,
both to the wise and the foolish" (Rom. 1:14). I am in
debt! You are in debt! Think about it — everything we
have and enjoy is the result of somebody else, or something else. The foundation has already been laid by others. *Wait a minute* you may be thinking. All right . . . I
challenge you to think of one thing you have done completely by yourself! Go ahead, I'll wait while you think.

Do I hear you mumbling, "But, I am a self-made person." And I'm sorry about that, too. If you are a self-
made person, why did you stop so soon?

If you don't have all the success you want in life, at
least be grateful for all the things you don't have that you
don't want!

A man is being chased by a tiger, he runs until he
comes to a sheer cliff. As the tiger bears down on him,
he grabs a rope hanging over the cliff and climbs down
out of the tiger's reach. He looks and sees the tiger growl-
ing at him. Then he looks down and sees a deadly drop
to the rocky floor about 500 feet below. Then he looks
up and sees two mice beginning to chew on the rope.
What should he do?

The tiger above, rocks below, the rope about to break!
Just then he spots a bright red, ripe strawberry growing
out of the side of the cliff. He stretches out his hand and
plucks the strawberry and pops it into his mouth. The
juices are so sweet that as he eats he can't contain himself and says, "Delicious, that's the very best strawberry I
ever tasted."

Had the man been preoccupied with the tiger (the PAST) or preoccupied with the rocks below (the FUTURE), he would never have enjoyed the strawberry, which we call "the gift of the PRESENT!

> ## NOTHING IN LIFE IS ENJOYABLE
> ## WITHOUT GRATITUDE!

In one part of Mexico a hot spring and a cold spring are found side by side. Because of the convenience of this natural phenomenon the women of the village often bring their laundry and boil their clothes in the hot spring and rinse them in the cold spring. A tourist, who was watching this procedure commented to his Mexican friend and guide, "I imagine that they think old Mother Nature is pretty generous to supply such ample, clean hot and cold water here side by side for their free use."

The guild replied, "No, senor, there is much grumbling because she supplies no soap."

Why the attitude of gratitude? For one thing it is commanded: "Give thanks in all circumstances!" In all circumstances includes your present situation. Note that it doesn't say "give thanks FOR all things" it says "IN all circumstances!"

This is the attitude which insures that all of life becomes a joy.

This incident happened in a nursing home. It was the annual Thanksgiving Day celebration special dinner. Tradition was observed when each resident at the table in turn expressed their thanks for one blessing. One little old lady said, "I thank God for two perfectly good teeth . . . and for the fact that one is in my upper and one is in my lower jaw so that I can chew."

Then . . . there was this preacher in our denomination who is completely bald, not a hair on his head. He was at a fellowship meeting in which people were given the opportunity to express their thanks. Oh, yes, his fellow colleagues had nicknamed him, "Mr. Clean." He stood to his feet and said, "I thank God for two perfectly good eyebrows."

IF YOU CAN'T BE GRATEFUL FOR WHAT YOU HAVE RECEIVED, AT LEAST BE GRATEFUL FOR THE THINGS YOU DIDN'T RECEIVE.

DEVELOP THE HABIT OF EXPRESSING GRATITUDE

Ungratefulness generally tends to be a sin of the rich. And we are very rich! Look at us! Look at what we wear, eat, drive, entertain, and live in. Compared to others in this world . . . we are rich beyond their fondest dream.

Take a kid who has never had anything of this world's goods and no hope of every having anything, who wakes up on Christmas morning in a humble tar-paper shack . . . to receive only one delicious apple for Christmas. Do you think he will be grateful for that apple?

In contrast, take another kid, same age, who wakes up every morning in a $750,000 house, who has never worked a day in his life, who puts hundreds of dollars worth of clothes on his back, wears the latest "Air Jordans," and drives his own red convertible to school. This kid complains at Christmas because the computer he's been given doesn't have all the software and games he wanted.

Possessive lust for things is a bottomless pit. Ingratitude becomes a curse to everyone who is consumed by it. The child treated to an ice cream cone complains because there are no sprinkles for the top like he wants . . . nothing is ever quite right for people who are gripped by the sin of ingratitude.

There are parents who scrimp and save and sacrifice just to be able to take their kids to Disneyland, which the kids think is their just due. It never dawns on the kids that their parents may be spending one of the worst vacations of their whole lives just so that the kids can have fun. These parents pay exorbitant prices for entry fees, motel rooms, and hot dogs that taste like stale sawdust; stand in long lines in the hot sun; go on rides that make them wish they were dead, who say to themselves, "I can't believe I am paying people to do this to me." At the end of the day, parents are exhausted and dead broke . . . but it's been worth it because the kids had their fun.

But the kids cry and complain because their parents won't stop by the movies on the way to the motel. And never offer a single word of thanks or appreciation to Mom and Dad. Not!

The child of God, the person in pursuit of success, must at some point in life be able to say to those around him, "This is much more than I deserve!" "Thank you, GOD! Thank you, Mom and Dad! Thank you, spouse! Thank you, kids! Thank you, fellow workers! Thank you, teachers and mentors! etc., etc., etc."

Ingratitude is a sin because it causes people to look inward, being unconcerned about others and what they have done or sacrificed. Ingratitude causes people to live in the bondage of self-centeredness, not able to enjoy any of life and success.

An Indian rajah had a gardener who was a chronic thief. This nobleman overlooked it for years because the gardener never stole anything of real value. One day, however, he stole a ruby which he had pried out of the royal crown and ran off in the night.

He stole the rajah's horse and raced out of the royal compound in the dark, trampling the nobleman's son and killing him. The rajah's soldiers captured the wretched thief and killer a few days later. He was hauled before the rajah. With the executioner's sword poised over his neck, the penitent thief cried out, "Please, mighty master, have mercy on me. Don't kill me. If not for my sake, then for my wife and kids. I plead. . . ."

The rajah forgave him of thievery and even the murder of his son and re-instated him as the gardener. Months later, the gardener was again hauled before the rajah. This time he had stolen a nearly worthless cup from the royal kitchen. The rajah said, "Bring the swordsman and cut his head off. Execute him here in my presence."

This time the gardener didn't plead for his life. Instead he said, "I deserve to die. I'm not complaining. But I don't understand . . . you forgive me for the death of your son and the theft of a ruby, then execute me for the theft of a miserable cup from your kitchen."

The rajah replied, "NO! No, you still don't understand. I'm not executing you for the theft of a cup. I'm having you executed for the sin of ingratitude."

Then, we have the American teen scene where one of life's critical issues has become the brand name on your tennis shoes or the label on your jeans. There are teens who would rather stay away from school than to show up in a K-Mart brand of tennis shoes!

But in many parts of the world, there are teens who might be praying, "O God, just once before I die, could I have a pair of shoes? Any kind!"

All ingratitude is basically a slap at God! The Bible reminds us that "every good gift and every perfect gift comes down from above" (James 1:17). God has given us health, food, clothing, a good house, a car to drive, a family to enjoy, and we complain because we are not the CEO of the Ford Motor Company. We pray for a job, then complain because it doesn't pay what we think we should be worth, while there are people who do almost anything to have a job. There are women who pray for a new home and then get angry because it takes too long to clean it, while others are praying for shelter. A single lady prays and prays and prays for a husband and then gets mad at God because the man is not perfect . . . and so it goes.

Living in gratitude as well as being ungrateful are simply habits of life. It is a way of life. It's living with an open hand instead of a clenched fist. It is saying "yours" and not "mine." It is sharing the spirit of Jesus Christ who freely gives to us all things. This expressing thanks is not a burden, in fact it makes the burdens of life much lighter. It is the joy of serving, giving, loving, and being that returns so much more to us than to the object of our thankfulness. It's not a burdensome duty. It is the joy and attitude of life that makes the inner person dance in delight!

Dr. Robert Cade is a research physician at the University of Florida. In 1965 he was asked why football players lose so much weight during extended practices and games. That question led to research in which Cade developed a drink designed to replenish the fluids lost during heavy exercise. He even named the drink after the Florida football team: "GATORADE"!

Last year, the Stokley-Van Camp company had Gatorade sales of more than $400 MILLION! Dr. Cade's royalties have provided him with a tremendous income. Yet he still lives in the same house in Gainesville, preferring to use his money on behalf of others. He has supported Vietnamese boat people, paid the bills of many needy hospital patients, funded research performed to help others, and currently underwrites the education of 16 medical students.

When asked about his giving and his lifestyle, he replied: "God has blessed me in all kinds of ways, including a big income. In the Book of Deuteronomy, God tells the Israelites a man should give as he is blessed. I think I am duty-bound to do as He suggests as an expression of gratitude."[12]

Let the peace of God rule in your
hearts, since as members of one body you
were called to peace. AND BE THANKFUL
(Col. 3:15, emphasis added).

Gratitude from the heart is the antidote to the selfish
spirit of this age! There is an attitude of today which cries
out, "More, more, more . . . me, mine, myself." The attitude of thankfulness makes for the joy in the journey, the
dance in the spirit, the upbeat in the heart, the lift for the
day, the oil of gladness to counter the sand in the gears
of living!

IT ISN'T WHAT YOU HAVE IN YOUR BANK
ACCOUNT THAT MAKES YOU THANKFUL . . .
BUT WHAT YOU HAVE IN YOUR HEART!

Chapter 12

True Success and the Blessing Principle

*A true friend will bless you with love,
strengthen you with prayer, and
encourage you with hope!*

Would you really like to be supernaturally blessed in
your relationships, your home, your emotions, your
health, and your finances? Would you like to have your
life filled with peace, with joy that is unspeakable, and to
live in a victorious mode? Sure! Who wouldn't?

Here is another of those little-known, supposedly
hidden "secrets" on how to live successfully. It's obvious
. . . too often overlooked. The young Mrs. Pollock, push-
ing a baby buggy with two baby boys in it, encountered
Mrs. Miller, who was also out for a morning walk. Mrs.
Miller said, "Good morning, Mrs. Pollock. My, what beautiful boys! So . . . how old are they?"

"The doctor," said Mrs. Pollock, "is two. The lawyer,
bless his heart, tomorrow is his first birthday."

Just keep this simple little exchange in the back of
your mind as we make our way through this important,
final principle on experiencing success without any guilt.

The "secret" we are talking about is the supernatural power of the "blessing." This is another of those biblical mysteries that have been lost to most of us for the past 2,000 years or more. However . . . it is a mystery that the Jewish people have been practicing consistently from the time of Abraham! We desperately need to re-discover this truth and put these principles into practice.

When somebody near to you sneezes . . . what do you say in reply? Sure . . . we all do it. "God bless you!" Right? We have said it so often and without thinking that we don't have a clue as to its significance or meaning. Blessings can take all kinds of forms and, when you think about it, the principle has been practiced by many others. Perhaps you remember this old Irish blessing:

> May you be in heaven 30 minutes be-
> fore the devil knows you're dead.

When you say, "I bless you in the name of the Lord," it is much more than simply words. Many of us, when we think of blessings, are reminded of the goodness of God in blessing us . . . rarely of the privilege of blessing others.

> The Lord said to Moses, "Tell Aaron
> and his sons, 'This is how you are to bless
> the Israelites. Say to them: The Lord bless
> you and keep you; the Lord make his face
> shine upon you and be gracious to you;
> the Lord turn his face toward you and give
> you peace. So they will put my name on
> the Israelites, and I WILL BLESS THEM!
> (Num. 6:22-27).

IT IS GOD'S WILL TO BLESS YOU . . . NOT
BECAUSE YOU DESERVE IT, BUT BECAUSE IT IS
THE VERY NATURE OF GOD TO BLESS!

God does not love you nor bless you, because of what you do or not do. (It is true that some of God's blessings are conditional.) God blesses you because He has chooses to. God is God and God is love! He loves you because He is love and it is His nature to love! In the plan of God it is your responsibility and privilege to bless others in His name, too! As you experience success of any kind it is incumbent that such blessings be passed on to others, as we have discovered previously. But when we talk of receiving a blessing and passing it along, we are taking this principle and concept to another level.

WHAT IS THE "BLESSING"?

Let's start with a working definition of the "blessing." A blessing is the impartation of the supernatural power of God into a human life as spoken by a delegated authority of God. We can expand that to bless is to . . . consecrate or sanctify, to request of God the bestowal of divine favor on a person, to bestow good of any kind upon others, and to protect from any kind of evil.

We must acknowledge that words have life and power. When spoken as a spiritual authority, you can literally shape the destiny of others! This is an exciting subject . . . so let's expand on it a bit further.

We can define a blessing as . . .

> to make whole or holy by the spoken word,
> to ask for Divine favor for someone else,
> to wish a person or situation well,
> to make prosperous,
> to make another happy or glad!

The very first blessing which was recorded comes on the first page of the Bible. It was the first act of God following the creation of the first couple. "Male and female He created them. God blessed them" (Gen. 1:27-28). The very first thing! A blessing pronounced on the first husband

and wife, on the very first home which was established, on the very first human relationship! I happen to think this must have been a priority. Following the blessing came three commands: "Be fruitful and increase in number . . . subdue it . . . rule over" it! The blessing enabled what was to follow creation.

The second recorded pronouncing of a blessing was spoken by God to Abraham: "I will make you into a great nation and I will bless you; I will make your name great, and you will be a blessing. I will bless those who bless you, and whoever curses you I will curse; and all peoples on earth will be blessed through you" (Gen. 12:2-3). Here is one absolutely, indisputable spiritual law of sowing and reaping. It works for you or against you! Notice the progression . . . God blessed Abraham first, which in turn made him a blessing to others, and anyone who also blessed Abraham would in turn be blessed. There was a negative side . . . whoever curses you will be cursed. And because of the blessings of God in the life of Abraham, all people, everywhere would also share in the blessings!

The application is simple . . . when God has blessed you or me, we are to bless others because there is also the possibility that many others would also be blessed in the process. As God blessed Abraham, Abraham was able to also bless others. It's a two-way street.

OUR BUSINESS!

We are not storerooms, but channels;
We are not cisterns, but springs;
Passing our benefits onward,
Fitting our blessings with wings;

Letting the water flow outward
To spread o'er the desert forlorn.
Sharing our bread with our brothers,
Our comfort with those who mourn.

(Author is unknown)

As previously stated, the Jewish people have largely employed this principle of blessing from the time of Abraham's day to today. Each Sabbath, as is their custom and as a part of their worship, Jewish mothers and fathers bless their children in the name of the God of Abraham, Isaac, and Jacob. When these boys and girls reach the age of 13, there is a special celebration marking the passing out of childhood into adulthood called a "bar mitzvah" for boys and a "bat mitzvah" for girls. During this wonderful ceremony, before the assembled congregation, parents place their hands on their 13 year old and bless them publicly. What are they saying and why are they doing this? They are literally shaping the destiny and future of their children, who now at age 13 are considered adults. They are molding what they want their children to be in their future years and living. It's powerful. (Recall our opening illustrative story.)

Do you happen to know any Jewish people who are not blessed? Yes, I know there may be some. But have you noticed the many who have been successful in finance, medicine, science, or commerce? Could the "blessing" be one of their keys to success? I happen to believe that it is. Because as a race and as a group of people, they are successful in all kinds of endeavors out of proportion to their numbers. Parents blessing their children so that those children believe and receive this blessing to go out into life and put into practice the power of the blessing. The impartation of the blessing gives something special to the life of every Jewish child.

A bearded old man once patted the head of ten-year-old Leo Rosten and chuckled fondly: "You look like a nice boy. I bless you with long life so you should live to 121."

Later, when he told his father, his father explained, "Jews say that because Moses lived to be 120."

"Oh, but why did the old man tell me 121?"

Rosten's father smiled and replied, "Maybe he didn't

want you to die suddenly."

Now contrast this kind of living to the Gentile neighbors down the block who are telling their kids, "You're stupid . . . you'll never amount to anything . . . why can't you get this right?" Meanwhile, the Goldbergs across the street are telling their children and blessing their children with dreams, "Go out and conquer the world as you are blessed of God!" And these blessed kids are doing it. Jewish parents continually pronounce the positive blessings over their kids and their living.

Which do you want? Do you want to impart the blessings and dreams of God into your kids or do you want to poison their future by your words? Whether you bless or curse . . . there are consequences!

Here is how it was lived out in the life of a sister who was about to leave forever:

> So they sent their sister Rebekah on her way, along with her nurse and Abraham's servant and his men and they blessed Rebekah and said to her, "Our sister, may you increase to thousands upon thousands; may your offspring possess the gates of their enemies" (Gen. 24:59-60).

That is powerful! And if you read on in her history . . . you will discover that it came to pass!

When the head of a biblical family pronounced a verbal blessing, it was taken as a very serious matter. People were ready to kill to receive this special first blessing. "Esau held a grudge against Jacob because of the blessing his father had given him" (Gen. 27:41). And you can continue on to read about the whole sordid story of how this blessing was stolen and could not be retrieved.

Let's talk about Jesus Christ and "the blessing."

He began His earthly ministry by delivering the most famous sermon ever preached. We call it the "Sermon on the Mount." His introduction included nine blessings pronounced on all who will participate in living life by these principles. He said, "Blessed are the poor in spirit . . . blessed are those who mourn . . . blessed are the meek . . . blessed are those who hunger . . . blessed are the merciful . . . blessed are the pure in heart . . . blessed are the peacemakers . . . blessed are those who are persecuted because of righteousness . . . blessed are you when people insult you" (Matt. 5:3-11). These are nine powerful blessings that will shape the destiny and future of all who follow these concepts for successful living.

In the Jewish tradition, it was the older person who blessed the younger person by placing a right hand on the younger and speaking those words of blessing. It was the leader who was to bless the follower, the parent who was to bless the child. So we see a most interesting scene with Jesus interrupting His teaching to the adults who were following Him to take the time to bless the children in the crowd: "He took the children in His arms, put his hands on them and blessed them" (Mark 10:14).

If Jesus blessed the children . . . why don't we? What did He say as He blessed them? We do not have a recording about what He said, but I would suspect that what He said would have been patterned after the blessing command given in Numbers 6.

The last thing Jesus did while still on this earth was to raise up His hands. Let's read, so we get it right:

> When He had led them out to the vicinity of Bethany, He lifted up His hands and blessed them. While He was blessing them, He left them and was taken up into heaven" (Luke 24:50-51).

His first and last priority was to bless others! If He did it . . . why don't we? If He is to be our example, why don't we do it?

THE POWER OF THE BLESSING!

There is so much unexplored territory when dealing with this subject. I had never thought of this concept nor had ever read about it until a friend of mine
pointed out the biblical concept. Then, upon research-
ing . . . it was obvious. It's everywhere in the Book! It's
a practice which has been overlooked and understated.
I believe it needs to be re-discovered as a principle of
living that can have a powerful impact on each of us
individually and collectively as we begin to unleash the
power of the blessing.

"BLESS those who persecute you; BLESS and do not
curse!" (Rom. 12:14, emphasis added). Right here is one
of those overlooked life principles. Why should we bless
and not curse? So we can demonstrate how good we
are? Not necessarily . . . but it is to demonstrate that we
have overcome evil with good. There's power and protection in blessing instead of cursing a situation or person. When you bless you provide a hedge, an invisible
shield over yourself. When you curse another . . . likely
you will be cursed in return. Where does it end? It causes
all kinds of bitterness to take root deep in the human
soul . . . then all joy and peace is gone.

In the Bible, the right hand symbolized the greater
blessing and the left hand the lesser blessing or the curse.
You may recall the story that when Jacob was to bless
two of his grandchildren, Joseph's first and second born,
he reversed his hands, crossed his hands, and pronounced
the greater right-handed blessing on the younger and
the lesser or left-handed blessing on the older. Joseph
noticed and tried to stop him but Jacob in so many words
said, "Leave me alone, I know what I am doing." Because of the power of the blessing, Joseph wanted it to
go to his oldest.

This little incident is a type or picture of what happened when Jesus was dying on the cross. In essence it

was as though the Heavenly Father was placing the left hand of cursing on Jesus and the right hand of blessing on all of us so that we might receive the benefits of His death and suffering. Think about this:

> Christ redeemed us from the curse of the law by becoming a curse for us, for it is written: Cursed is everyone who is hung on a tree. He redeemed us in order that the blessing given to Abraham might come to the Gentiles so that by faith we might receive the promise (Gal. 3:13-14).

In the Old Testament of the Bible, the only way you could become a part of the priesthood was by birth, a natural birth into the tribe of Levi. Today, the only way you can become a part of the present day priesthood is also by birth, the new birth, by being born again. And by being a part of this priesthood, you have the power and authority to pronounce blessing upon others. When you have been blessed with godly success . . . you also have the obligation and privilege of passing it on to others. You can bless others with your material goods, with your powerful knowledge, with your love, and all of God's best. So . . . bless and don't curse!

THE PERMANENCE OF THE BLESSING!

Once a blessing was spoken into existence it could not be broken by another person. It could be stopped by God because of disobedience, but not by other humans. The truth of this is found in the sad story of old, blind, and feeble Isaac who is being deceived by his younger son, Jacob, so he could receive the blessing, the blessing reserved for the oldest son. As you read this pathetic story, this chapter ends with these forlorn words, "I have blessed Jacob and he will be blessed . . . once it has been given, I cannot take it back!"

If you are a parent, be careful what you speak as you begin to shape the destiny of your children. There is a permanence about the spoken word. Words can help or hinder, lift or put down, heal or hurt. They will be remembered for a lifetime by your kids.

Later in the life of Jacob, when he is old and about to die, he called his 12 sons and spoke into each of their lives a blessing. Take the time to read through all these blessings as recorded in Genesis 49 and you will be amazed to see how closely each of these 12 sons lived them out exactly as their father had spoken these words.

When Jesus was still on this earth He had 12 disciples. He told them that they were the light of the world, the salt of this earth, and world-changers. At the point in time when He first pronounced these words . . . they were anything but. They were filled with imperfections and flaws.

Simon Peter, who was probably the most flawed, except for Judas, later became a powerful light in this world. The point is that they rose to the LEVEL OF THE BLESSING! They literally became what He had said because He shaped their destinies with the power and permanence of the blessing! I know that there were other factors involved . . . but you must agree with me that the pronouncements Jesus spoke played a powerful role in their future lifestyle.

PRONOUNCING THE BLESSING!

In the Old Testament the priests were responsible to bless the people. But today, who are the "priests" in the New Testament plan? Read the following carefully and thoroughly:

But YOU are a chosen people, a ROYAL
PRIESTHOOD, a holy nation, a people be-

> longing to God, that you may declare the
> praises of Him who called you out of dark-
> ness into His wonderful light (1 Pet. 2:9).

YOU are chosen, YOU are a part of the royal priest-hood, YOU! Yes, YOU! What was one of the responsibilities of the priesthood? To pronounce blessings on others! Since we are called of God to this royal priesthood we should begin to practice what we are told to do, a practice which has been lost for too long. Instead of whining, cursing, complaining, or gossiping . . . start blessing what you need, start blessing those who persecute you, start blessing others! Pronounce blessings and not cursings! We are told to bless and not to curse!

There are at least three things we can bless according to the Bible:

1. We can BLESS situations and circumstances! If there is any unsold merchandise at your store, start blessing it instead of complaining. If you don't like your present job, circumstances, salary, health, or church . . . start blessing these things in His name!

2. We can BLESS people! Start by blessing your spouse, your kids, your parents, your grandparents, your aunts and uncles . . . yes, even the difficult ones! If they are not living like you think they should, start blessing them, start pronouncing God's blessings over them. Once you have started, don't stop with one blessing, continue.

3. We can BLESS the Lord God of this universe! As you begin to learn the secrets and joys of this life discipline, instead of complaining or cursing, you most naturally will begin to bless the Lord who is the source of all good blessings! David wrote, "Bless the Lord, oh my soul and all that is within me, bless His holy name" (Ps. 101:1).

This is one of the most powerful life-giving concepts. About now, if you are like me, you may be asking, "What should I say when pronouncing a blessing on someone else?" Here is a listing of at least 30 things which you can say in blessing others, as taken from the Bible:

1. God bless you with ability!
2. God bless you with abundance!
3. God bless you with clear direction!
4. God bless you by sending His angels to go with you!
5. God bless you with His assurance of His love and His grace and His mercy!
6. God bless you with a controlled and disciplined life!
7. God bless you with courage!
8. God bless you with creativity!
9. God bless you with a spiritual perception of God's truth!
10. God bless you with faith!
11. God bless you with God's favor and with man's favor!
12. God bless you with good health!
13. God bless you with a good wife or a good husband!
14. God bless your hands so you can bless others!
15. God bless you with happiness!
16. God bless you with fulfillment!
17. God bless you with contentment!
18. God bless you with hope and a good outlook on life!
19. God bless you with a listening ear!
20. God bless you with a long life!
21. God bless you with an obedient heart to the Spirit of God!
22. God bless you with His peace!
23. God bless you with pleasant speech!
24. God bless you with a pleasant personality!
25. God bless you with promotion!
26. God bless you with protection!

27. God bless you with provision, safety, and strength!
28. God bless you with trust and wisdom!
29. God bless you with success!
30. God bless you with goodness and mercy following you all the days of your life so that you might dwell in the house of the Lord forever!

Absolutely powerful, awesome!

Perhaps we need to pause and simply digest some of the above, to count the blessings of God in our own life. Do you know anybody whom you can bless in His Name? How about starting with your enemies, your family, your associates? Have you been counting?

The hostess was making her rounds at the special tea for ladies, with a platter of freshly baked, homemade cookies. "So, Mrs. Pearlstein," she smiled, "have some cookies."

"No thank you," said Mrs. Pearlstein. "They're absolutely delicious . . . but I already had four."

"You already had FIVE," said the hostess, "but who's counting?"

> The blessings we evoke for another descend upon ourselves! (Edmund Gibson)

THE FIVE BLESSINGS YOU AND OTHERS NEED

We have talked more in terms of giving or pronouncing a blessing on others . . . a sharing of our own success as spoken into someone else's life. But let's turn this a bit for a look at the blessings needed by all of us in order to experience all that life and success may hold for us.

Read this blessing as pronounced by God:

> I will make a covenant of peace. . . . I will bless them and the places surrounding my hill. I will send down showers in

season; there will be showers of blessing.
The trees of the field will yield their fruit
and the ground will yield its crops; the
people will be secure in their land. They
will know that I am the Lord, when I break
the bars of their yoke and rescue them from
the hands of those who have enslaved
them (Ezek. 34:25-27).

1. ELIJAH'S BLESSING: It's simply this: "God will provide when there is a need!" You will find this story of
provision in 1 Kings 17. It's a story of Elijah, a weary,
worn-out, burned-out prophet in desperate need. God
provides with ravens who bring him daily food beside a
clear babbling brook for a water source, and divine sleep,
courtesy of an angel sent by God. Later in this story we
watch as Elijah speaks to a widow in Zarephath, giving
her instructions on how she is to survive the famine in
the land by her obedience. So she and her son, as well as
the prophet, survive on the miraculously provided supply of oil and flour. My friend, God knows what your needs
are and when they are needed. GOD WILL PROVIDE!

2. SOLOMON'S BLESSING: This man was able to tap
into the divine supply of wisdom. "Wisdom from on high!"
How are we to get wisdom? Ask God, for that is the
starting place. THEN, determine and discipline yourself
to live by these godly principles (Prov. 9:10; 8:17-21).
Solomon became the wisest man on the face of the earth,
other than Jesus Christ. He lived by these concepts, as
God also blessed him with this wisdom which was followed by success and material blessings of all kinds, beyond anything we can imagine. However, there is a sad
ending to this story. The man who was the wisest among
men in his later years broke all the proverbs he had so
carefully recorded and written.

3. ABRAHAM'S BLESSING: "Your children will be
blessed and will bless others!" For the background on

this blessing you can refer to Genesis 22:17-18, 20. Yes, Abraham was blessed with many things . . . for example, his name was changed from Abram to Abraham. And when his name was changed, his life was changed. God took the "H" from His own name, "Jehovah" and put it into Abram's name making him an Abraham reflecting the very characteristics of God to others. Part of the blessing of Abraham was the way in which God blessed him because of his obedience.

4. DANIEL'S BLESSING: "You will survive!" Has life put you into a den of lions? My friend, you will survive! King Darius wrote a special decree declaring that "He rescues and He saves; He performs signs and wonders in the heavens and on the earth. He has rescued Daniel from the power of the lions" (Dan. 6:27). Does it seem as though there is no way out for you at this moment? There is a God in heaven who still delivers, who still can shut up the mouths of hungry lions, who is willing to show His strength and power on behalf of those who have put their trust in Him!

5. JOB'S BLESSING: "The later years are the greater years!" This Book of Job is not only a story about the survival of one man who was severely tested without knowing what the testing and disaster was all about, it's also the story of how God blessed a business man. It's the story of a "plan B" in action, of how this man came back from the brink of financial disaster, of how this man who survived the testing to rise from the ash heap of disaster, in the end experienced twice the material and family blessings he had before the trial came his way. It's amazing that this, the oldest book in the Bible is about a businessman surviving disaster and the last part of his life being doubly blessed. I think that is significant.

You also need to know that the words "bless, blessed, blessings," and other variations, are found approximately 550 times in the Bible. This is a huge subject which needs more study and a practical life application. It is wonderful to be blessed of God as well as to bless others in His name! Both aspects are exciting. Think of how long any of us could survive without the blessings of God evident in our living.

> David says the same thing when he speaks of the BLESSEDNESS of the man to whom God credits righteousness apart from works:
> BLESSED are they whose transgressions are forgiven, whose sins are covered.
> BLESSED is the man whose sin the Lord will never count against him (Rom. 4:6-8, emphasis added).

We follow that up with these powerful words spoken by a man named Balak who had no doubts as to the powerfulness and positiveness of our subject:

> I know that those you bless are blessed, and those you curse are cursed (Num. 22:6).

I don't know about you, but I, for one, want my life to be lived in such a way so that the blessings of God will come upon me and overtake me! It is possible to position yourself in such a way through obedience that you cannot possibly avoid the blessings of God. There are many life actions which will cause these blessings of God to be ours. Hear it carefully:

> If you fully obey the Lord your God and carefully follow all His commands I give you today, THE LORD YOUR GOD WILL SET YOU HIGH ABOVE ALL THE NATIONS ON THE EARTH. ALL THESE BLESSINGS WILL COME UPON YOU AND ACCOMPANY YOU IF YOU OBEY THE LORD YOUR GOD

(Deut. 28:1-2, emphasis added).

My recommendation to you is that you take the time, right now, to read through the entire chapter of Deuteronomy 28. There are blessings for obedience and curses for disobedience. As simple as that. If you obey you will be blessed . . . if you disobey you will be cursed. And it follows that I do not want to be cursed of God.

How does this work out in real life? The principle is re-stated in the last book of the Old Testament and it still works today. Do you really want to open the windows of heaven so that you will receive blessings of heaven?

> Bring the whole tithe into the store-house, that there may be food in my house. Test me in this, says the Lord Almighty, and see if I will not throw open the flood-gates of heaven and pour out SO MUCH BLESSING THAT YOU WILL NOT HAVE ROOM ENOUGH FOR IT (Mal. 3:10, emphasis added).

But there's more, there's a bottom-line reason for God to bless you, to open His floodgates of blessing . . . so that "You will again see the distinction between the righteous and the wicked, between those who serve God and those who do not" (Mal. 3:18). Isn't it significant that God ends the Old Testament on this kind of a note? The Book of Genesis began with God pronouncing a blessing on the first pair created. . . . He also ends the book with another pronouncement of blessing on all those who are obedient to His concepts!

The apostle Paul really has the bottom line on this subject as he speaks a final word to the elders of the church in Ephesus. He concludes with these lines:

> In everything I did, I showed you that
> by this kind of hard work we must help the

weak, remembering the words the Lord
Jesus himself said: IT IS MORE BLESSED TO
GIVE THAN TO RECEIVE (Acts 20:35, em-
phasis added).

Pastor Bill Simpson writes the following: What is your
most memorable Thanksgiving? For me, it was on the
eve of the day. The church had the names of ten families
scheduled to receive food baskets. A local merchant do-
nated hams, and groceries were purchased. As we packed
these boxes in our fellowship hall, these families were
excited over the food they were taking home. As they
were picking up their boxes, another family arrived. Father, mother, and three kids piled out of an old pickup
and came inside the hall. This was a new family not on
our list. They had just heard there was food being distrib-
uted by a church.

I explained that we did not have enough for an extra
family . . . and as I tried to assure them that I would do
what I could, an amazing thing happened. With no
prompting, a woman put down the box she was carrying
and quickly found an empty box to place beside it. She
began removing items from her box to share. Soon others followed her lead and these ten poor families created
an 11th box for the new family!

There is one Christian man who realized that he had
never received a blessing from his aging father. So he
went to his non-Christian father and asked his dad to bless
him. His father was hesitant . . . then finally responded, "I
guess so, son. But I don't really know what to do or how
to say a blessing."

The son replied, "It's not hard, Dad. Just think what
you wish would happen with me and my family and speak
those words over me."

As the father began, his words were faltering. But as
his thoughts became clear, his words of blessing began

to be poured out. The blessing flowed freely as did the tears. That day for the first time, father and son bonded and remained close until the day the father died.

Who is the son? He is the Reverend John Kilpatrick, pastor of the Brownsville Assembly of God church in Pensacola, Florida. Pastor Kilpatrick has stated that rediscovering the principles of the blessing have been one of the most significant and important elements that have come into the life of their church.

I want to end this book with the priestly blessing, much like the one Pastor Kilpatrick shared with his church, spoken over his congregation week after week. It is taken from the Bible. Take it, listen carefully, receive it, read it over and over as you continue on in your quest of real, true success without guilt!

IN THE NAME OF JESUS CHRIST . . . I bless you with the promises of God that are "YES" and "AMEN!"

The Holy Spirit make you healthy and strong in body, mind, and spirit to move in faith and expectancy!

May God's angels be with you to protect and keep you!

Be blessed with supernatural strength to turn your eyes from foolish, worthless, and evil things. Instead, may you behold the beauty of things that God has planned for you as you obey His word!

I bless your ears to hear the lovely, the uplifting, and the encouraging, and to shut out the demeaning and the negative!

May your feet walk in holiness and your steps be ordered by the Lord!

May your hands be tender helping hands to those in need, hands that bless!

May your heart be humble and receptive to one another, and to the things of God and not to the world!

May your mind be strong, disciplined, balanced, and faith-filled!

God's grace be upon your home, that it may be a sanctuary of rest and renewal, a haven of peace where sounds of joy and laughter grace its walls, where love and unconditional acceptance of one another is consistent!

God give you success and prosperity in your business and places of labor as you acknowledge and obey the imperative of scripture concerning the tithe!

God give you spiritual strength to overcome the evil one and avoid temptation!

God's grace be upon you to fulfill your dreams and visions!

May goodness and mercy follow you all the days of your long life!

THE LORD BLESS YOU AND KEEP YOU!

THE LORD MAKE HIS FACE SHINE UPON YOU, AND BE GRACIOUS UNTO YOU!

THE LORD LIFT UP HIS COUNTENANCE UPON YOU AND GIVE YOU PEACE!

I BLESS YOU IN JESUS' NAME!!!

(A special note of thanks goes to Alton Garrison, pastor of First Assembly of God in North Little Rock for his kind help in writing this last chapter. Thanks for the inspiration and valuable research which has made this final chapter a reality.)

Endnotes

1 Dennis Waitley, *The Double Win*, (Old Tappan, NJ: Fleming H. Revell Co., 1985), p. 41-43, adapted).

2 Zig Ziglar, condensed.

3 *Christianity Today*, April 15, 1985.

4 Gretchen Gaebelein Hull, *Christianity Today*, September 21, 1985, p. 14 - 18.

5 Tim Hansel, *When I Relax I Feel Guilty* (Colorado Springs, CO: David C. Cook Pub. Co., 1979), p. 89.

6 Charles R. Swindoll, *Living Above the Level of Mediocrity* (Waco, TX: Word Books, 1987), p. 114.

7 *The Arizona Republic*, 4/25/95.

8 James Conner, AP, 5/23/84.

9 William Sadler, *Practice of Psychiatry* (St. Louis, MO: C.V. Mosby Co., 1953), p. 1008.

10 Shakespeare, *Macbeth*, v. 3, 38, 40.

11 Albert Camus, *The Fall*.

12 *Main Event*, September 1989, p. 24 (a sports journal for doctors).

Also from Robert Strand . . .

365 Moments to Cherish
Uplifting Stories to Bless the Heart, Strengthen the Home, and Deepen the Faith

With 750,000 of his "Moments to Give" series in print, author Robert Strand has now compiled the stories from that blockbuster series into one great book.

Filled with wonderfully inspirational true stories from among his books focusing on mothers, fathers, friends, grandparents (12 volumes in the series), this unique product follows the calendar as we celebrate events like Valentine's Day, Mother's Day, Teacher Appreciation Day, graduation, Grandparent's Day, Christmas, etc. A year's worth of cherished moments, this book is a must for gift givers and receivers! Also includes new stories. $14.95

Available at bookstores nationwide or contact
New Leaf Press • P.O. Box 726 • Green Forest, AR 72638